Wittgenstein Reads Freud

NEW FRENCH THOUGHT

SERIES EDITORS

Thomas Pavel and Mark Lilla

Jacques Bouveresse

Wittgenstein Reads Freud

THE MYTH OF THE UNCONSCIOUS

Translated by Carol Cosman

With a Foreword by Vincent Descombes

 NEW FRENCH THOUGHT

PRINCETON UNIVERSITY PRESS · PRINCETON, NEW JERSEY

Copyright © 1995 by Princeton University Press
Published by Princeton University Press, 41 William Street,
Princeton, New Jersey 08540
In the United Kingdom: Princeton University Press, Chichester, West Sussex

Translated from the French edition of Jacques Bouveresse, *Philosophie, mythologie et pseudo-science: Wittgenstein lecteur de Freud* (Paris: © 1991 Editions de l'éclat, 30250 Combas)

Library of Congress Cataloging-in-Publication Data

Bouveresse, Jacques.
[Philosophie, mythologie et pseudo-science. English]
Wittgenstein reads Freud : the myth of the
unconscious / Jacques Bouveresse ; translated by
Carol Cosman ; with a foreword by Vincent Descombes.
p.   cm.— (New French thought)
Includes bibliographical references (p.   ) and index.
ISBN 0-691-03425-7 (cloth)
ISBN 0-691-029040 (pbk.)
1. Psychoanalysis and philosophy.   2. Wittgenstein. Ludwig, 1889-1951—
Views on psychoanalysis.   3. Freud, Sigmund, 1856-1939—Influence.
4. Freud, Sigmund, 1856-1939.   I. Title.   II. Series.
BF175.4.P45B6813   1991
150.19′52—dc20   94-40607   CIP

Published with the assistance of the French Ministry of Culture

This book has been composed in Adobe Bauer Bodoni

Princeton University Press books are printed on acid-free paper and meet the guidelines
for permanence and durability of the Committee on Production Guidelines for Book
Longevity of the Council on Library Resources

Printed in the United States of America

10 9 8 7 6 5 4

Contents

Foreword

BY VINCENT DESCOMBES

IN ITS ORIGINAL VERSION, Jacques Bouveresse's essay on Wittgenstein and psychoanalysis bears both a title and a subtitle, each of them unusually explicit: *Philosophy, Mythology, and Pseudo-Science: Wittgenstein Reads Freud*. The subtitle, *Wittgenstein Reads Freud*, defines the book's subject—namely, Wittgenstein's judgments on Freud and, more generally, his attitude toward the man and his enterprise. The title, *Philosophy, Mythology, and Pseudo-Science*, announces the ultimate thrust of the entire discussion by introducing three intellectual categories: a new idea can come from either *philosophy*, *mythology*, or *science*. We can see that among these three registers, which share responsibility for intellectual invention, science alone is opposed by a counterfeit called "pseudo-science." "Pseudo-philosophy" does not seem to be a term we can use, much as we might be tempted to when dealing with what we think is bad philosophy. But philosophical speculation is such that everything that claims to be philosophy *is* philosophy. The price of this unlimited tolerance is that bad philosophy is as philosophical as good philosophy. Wittgenstein might say that bad philosophy is even more philosophical than good: not more philosophical in the sense of more profound or more solid, but rather in the sense of more representative of the characteristic temptations of philosophy, such as wrongly generalizing from a privileged example, or confusing the particularities of a mode of expression with the higher laws of being. The case of mythology presents a somewhat different picture, for mythological production is not the result of a specialized activity. A myth is what is told as a myth and what is transmitted as a myth; hence, we would not know how to distinguish false mythology from true mythology. Here again, we would speak instead of poor or insipid mythology rather than pseudo-mythology.

The French title of Bouveresse's book does not require any explanation for a French reader, who would immediately understand why such questions were being posed in the context of French philosophy. And this is specifically the issue I would like to address on the occasion of the American translation, with the hope of assisting an intelligent reading of it. Indeed, the main subject of Bouveresse's discussion is handled quite straightforwardly and needs no particular introduction. Readers will find in this book just what they are looking for: first, an attentive commentary on all the texts in which Wittgenstein mentions Freud, his ideas, and his therapeutic technique; and second, a discussion of all the literature on the question (in German, English, and French). But the particular French context in which it was first written and received deserves some explanation.

When Wittgenstein is speaking, his judgments bear on psychoanalysis as Freud defined it and disseminated it. But when Bouveresse brings together all of Wittgenstein's texts under a title that entertains three possible designations that might be assigned to Freudian thought—philosophy, mythology, or pseudo-science—his own judgment embraces both the psychoanalysis that concerned Wittgenstein and the characteristically French psychoanalysis purveyed by Jacques Lacan, who, moreover, presented his entire enterprise as a "return to Freud."

Early in this century, French philosophers behaved much like their colleagues in other countries in the face of psychoanalysis. Some did not show the slightest interest in the new doctrines coming from Vienna; others presented serious criticisms of this or that point, generally on moral or psychological grounds; and still others recognized the power and novelty of Freudian ideas and tried to give them a philosophical interpretation. Among these last, the names Jean-Paul Sartre and Maurice Merleau-Ponty have figured most prominently. After the war, their review *Les Temps Modernes* would welcome contributions from several renowned psychoanalysts, such as O. Mannoni and J. B. Pontalis. Still, Sartre was harshly critical of Freud's psychology, especially his determinism, and Merleau-Ponty suggested that Freudian theory, which was too naturalistic for his taste, might be corrected with a phenomenology of human subjectivity.

On their side, the first French psychoanalysts did not belong to any particular intellectual current and did not attribute much importance to the opinions of philosophers. They turned elsewhere, to the intellectuals or writers of the avant-garde, and especially to the surrealists, whether they were loyal to André Breton or dissidents like Georges Bataille and Michel Leiris. The surrealists were sensitive to a Romantic strain they thought they detected in Freud because of his interest in dreams and madness. They freely interpreted his notions of infantile sexuality and repression to buttress their argument in favor of uninhibited passion. In their circles, the absence of explicit criticism sat well with a quite selective appropriation. Freud, whose conservative literary tastes were well known, received the homage of the French surrealists cautiously and refrained from granting them the support of his intellectual authority.

The young Lacan, even as he was beginning a career as a psychiatrist, had close friendships among the surrealists. Several of the texts he published before the war appeared in the review *Le Minotaure*, and we know that until the end of his life Lacan recognized only Salvador Dali and Luis Buñuel as his rivals. Lacan managed to reverse the relationship between psychoanalysis and philosophy. Henceforth, it would not be the psychoanalysts who had to explain their philosophical principles in the context of a philosophical discussion but rather the philosophers who would have to explain their reticence or lack of enthusiasm toward psychoanalysis.

Lacan adopted and molded to his own purposes the idea advanced by Freud that psychoanalysis had launched an enormous intellectual revolution, equal in scope to the discoveries of heliocentrism and natural selection.[1] By inscribing his name in the pantheon of subversive thinkers, right after Copernicus and Darwin, Freud was suggesting that psychoanalysis was not only a scientific hypothesis but the source of a cultural upheaval.

Certain new ideas provoke tidal waves, and when these reach certain proportions, we speak of an "intellectual upheaval." But as we know, there is a scale for measuring seismic activity, and this goes for the shakings of intellectual ground as well. We could say that certain new ideas are only new scientific hypotheses; there is, as we would say today, a change of paradigm in a field, but not yet an intellectual revolution. As for an intellectual revolution, it provokes the change of paradigm by transforming the very principles of reasoning in all disciplines. But this still leaves us among philosophers. Only when an intellectual revolution is also the source, or the sign, of a mental rupture and an overturning of values do we surpass the limits of all philosophy. Wittgenstein would say that we no longer aim at producing a change limited to the intellect but seek to provoke an authentic change of human attitudes; therefore a change of will. And this is just where Wittgenstein's judgment of psychoanalysis goes further than that of most philosophers.

Lacan explains that Freud did not fully understand the novelty of his own discovery, as if he had not completely perceived its radical nature. Quite possibly, Lacan thought that only his own version of the Freudian idea had finally managed to disengage it from its thralldom to biology. According to Freud, psychoanalysis would be the third and most important of the "decenterings" of man. But for Lacan, the Freudian revolution was in reality much more serious than the other two. If the "Copernican revolution" consists of saying that the earth does not have a privileged place at the center of the system, since that place is occupied by the sun, this revolution is not as radical as it might seem: it persists in "exalting the center," therefore in requiring a center of things. In reality, the Copernican revolution is perfectly compatible with traditional religion, as indeed it was soon understood. It would have been much more serious to announce that there is no center (by drawing conclusions from the fact that the "celestial revolutions" of the planets are elliptical, not circular).

As for Darwin, his theory is said to have been humiliating and degrading: man was the distant relative of higher mammals. But Lacan observes that the perceived Darwinian message is not that man is not a separate being. Quite the contrary: thanks to the idea of evolution, men believe all the more that they are "at the top of the heap."

What Freud put into question, according to Lacan, is the very possibility that human beings can claim to be the center of anything. The notion of the unconscious ought to be understood as bearing witness to the impossibility of anyone attaining what the philosophers call the state of satisfaction in harmony with the self (or, in speculative Hegelian terms, self-identity triumphing over all alienations and internal divisions). The human being is indeed a "subject," as the philosophers after Descartes have said: the human attribute par excellence is the power to say "I" (*ego cogito, ego sum*). But he is also a "divided subject": the subject does not emerge until he speaks, but when he speaks, he loses himself in language and is condemned to desire without being able to signify the object of his desire in an articulate message. The subject is therefore divided, due to his condition as a speaking being, between what he can ask in the language he shares with others, and what he continues to desire—which is always "something else." The transformation of Freudian psychoanalysis into Lacanian psychoanalysis is therefore an enormously interesting phenomenon from the viewpoint of philosophical questions that also arise in Wittgenstein.

Lacan wanted to straddle both sides of the fence: on one side, Freudian theory concerns science (and preferably hard science), but on the other it concerns madness. Lacan did not want to renounce either of these inspirations, which made it possible for his project to be described by François Roustang as the deliberate project of a "scientific delirium": a production that defies classification and indeed raises the question whether it should be regarded as a specimen of "pseudo-science" or of "mythology."[2] Far from expressing reservations with respect to what Sartre, Merleau-Ponty, Paul Ricoeur, and others called Freud's "scientism," Lacan always insisted on preserving that part of the founding heritage. The "science" claimed by the psychoanalyst must not be a mere rigorous discipline tempered by hermeneutic considerations; it must be modeled on mathematical physics. Roustang has, moreover, shown that all of Lacan's work, from the first sketchy, prewar ventures to the "mathemes" of his old age, is governed by a postulate that is never questioned: science consists only of being able to decompose the phenomenon in question into elementary units and to find algebraic formulas to express the fundamental correlations between these variables. Lacan declared, for example, in the seminar he gave at the Ecole Normale Superieure on rue d'Ulm in 1965–66, that it is absolutely false that Freud broke with the scientific ideas of his time (namely, the project to integrate psychology and physiology "in the mathematical terms determined by thermodynamics").[3] In reality, Freud never would have founded psychoanalysis had he not been, as we say, a "scientist." (Of course, Lacan simply *declared* that Freud had adhered in principle to a scientific program, and did not suggest that psychoanalytic theory had in practice reduced psychology to a physics of energies. His emphasis was clearly on the authority of science rather than on any effectively obtained results. The program obviously counted more than the actual work.)

Nonetheless, Lacan did not hesitate to grant Freud stature of a different kind. In another lecture to a group of philosophers, Lacan compared Freud to Erasmus, a writer held to be the exemplary representative of the humanities.[4] Erasmus, says Lacan, praised madness from the viewpoint of the Socratic adage "know thyself." Freud reconfigured the paths to this knowledge by teaching us that we should look for the truth about ourselves, not in the "ego" of the philosophers but in aberrations, dreams, caprices, phobias, bungled actions, and so on. Lacan pursues the comparison between these figures in a discussion of the history of the humanities. Erasmus and Freud each played a revolutionary role, he says, the first by participating in the movement of humanism, the second by proposing an interpretation of dreams and symptoms. In both cases, explains Lacan, we are dealing with man's relation to language (to the "signifier"). Erasmus overturned "the procedures of exegesis" by substituting the critical reading of the philologist for the allegorizing reading of the theologian; Freud discovered that the "id speaks" there where physicians before him saw in hysterical symptoms, slips, or bungled actions only physiological difficulties or failures of proper behavior. Yet one cannot modify "man's relation to the signifier" without "changing the course of his history," says Lacan. Here, Freudianism is no longer a stage in the movement of a scientific program, it is a revolution whose consequences are infinite: "Everything that concerns not only the human sciences but the fate of man, politics, metaphysics, literature, the arts, advertising, propaganda, and consequently economics, has been affected by it." We are dealing, in effect, with an intellectual enterprise that goes well beyond the statement of a scientific hypothesis or even the construction of a philosophical system.

In short, the French situation since the Second World War has been marked by rivalry between philosophers and psychoanalysts. They have challenged each other's intellectual authority in the Parisian marketplace, which has favored the formulation of increasingly ambitious and encompassing agendas. Lacan's role in this affair was to up the ante. After Lacan, it was no longer enough to treat Freud as a great philosopher; psychoanalysis now had to be granted the privilege of a philosophical construction transcending dialectical arguments or conceptual inventions.

This construction would be validated by the conjunction of experiment and formalization. Lacanian epistemologists are unperturbed by the fact that what might be called the experiment (the couch) does not have the slightest relationship to the formal schemas being proposed (the "algebraic" or "topological" schemas). They seem indifferent to the fact that their scientific formulas play no role in the particular interpretations produced by the psychoanalyst, or that their "experiments" cannot possibly lead to a modification or enrichment of the formulas. The most important thing for them, it seems, is *not* to do what inventive philosophers do when they propose a new way of representing familiar phenomena. For psychoanalysis to fulfill its aspirations and go beyond philosophy, it had to make evident the *reality* of unconscious processes whose existence was unsuspected. It had to convince us, as Althusser used to say, that Freud had discovered a new "continent," the continent of the unconscious.[5]

As we know, the hypothesis of the unconscious is the keystone of the entire Freudian conceptual apparatus: repression, symptoms, the etiology of neuroses, dreams, slips, and so on. It is therefore natural that from the outset this concept has been the focal point of frequent discussion. Did Freud present a scientific hypothesis, as he always maintained and as his disciples keep repeating? Or did he instead, as Wittgenstein believes, invent a "manner of speaking"? Bouveresse effectively demonstrates the gulf that separates the two Viennese thinkers on this point. In a sense, it is Freud who has a classic conception of science and rationality; his ideas on physics or on the scientific method are not very different from those of many members of the Vienna Circle. Wittgenstein, by contrast, has a more heterodox view.

From the point of view of a Freudian—and, even more, a Lacanian—it is very important that psychoanalysis should be a scientific theory; if it did not have the dignity of a "science," it *would* be merely a manner of speaking. I mean that the locution "manner of speaking" would of necessity be taken, by a disciple of Freudian ideas, as degrading. This is not necessarily the case for Wittgenstein: to offer a new manner of speaking or of conceiving things, to propose a new system of expression, is not to elaborate a scientific theory, but neither is it to produce an arbitrary construction. In fact, there is something inventive and ingenious (indeed, verging on genius) in seizing upon a powerful image and setting it up as an *Urphänomen* for an entire class of facts. Where Wittgenstein's diagnosis becomes tinged with condemnation is when a systematic confusion is revealed between science, an activity that must be subject to empirical control, and the imaginative activity of inventing a system of notation. This claim to global explanation is the mark of pseudo-science.

Bouveresse has presented in his study all the passages of Wittgenstein's corpus (or of his primary disciples) that touch on psychoanalysis. It is important that Wittgenstein's judgments rarely bear on Freud's work alone but simultaneously on the reception of that work in contemporary culture, as if psychoanalysis were in the first instance a collective phenomenon before being the original idea of an individual thinker. It is not enough to wonder, for example, if Freud really gives "causal explanations," or if he ever gave reasons for thinking that his particular interpretations had been corroborated by facts worthy of the name. For Wittgenstein it is equally important to note that psychoanalysis is symptomatic of the times. That Freud regarded his theory as scientific is a fact that belongs to the intellectual biography of this thinker. But that the majority of people may believe it and voluntarily rank Freudianism among "scientific discoveries" says something profound about the times.

Here again we encounter the problem of how to distinguish a scientific theory from mythology. What is the defining feature of mythology? A classical rationalist or a positivist would answer that a mythological explanation is coarse or primitive. Wittgenstein rejects this notion. He does not in the least think that the "primitives" treated by Frazer are coarse, or that they reason less well than the celebrated author of *The Golden Bough*.[6] Therefore, mythology cannot be distinguished from science the way that the knowledge of ignorant people can be from that of scientists. The difference between them is not a matter of ages of the mind, as the philosophers of history believed. In fact, mythological explanation is not an attempt at scientific explanation, therefore partial and fallible. It can be recognized above all by its encompassing and imperious qualities: it is imposing, it elicits unconditional adherence and rejects in advance all possibility of disagreement on the basis of experiment. It persuades the mind that things must happen in a particular way, even if things seem to happen quite differently.

My super-ego might say of my ego: "It is raining, and the ego believes so," and might go on "So I shall probably take an umbrella with me." And now how does this game go on?

—LUDWIG WITTGENSTEIN,
Remarks on the Philosophy of Psychology,
vol I, sec. 708

T HIS WORK is adapted from two studies published some years ago: "Wittgenstein face à la psychanalyse," which appeared in the journal *Austriaca*,[1] and "Wittgenstein et Freud," in *Vienne au tournant du siècle*.[2] My purpose here is to come to a better understanding of the sometimes enigmatic remarks Wittgenstein made about psychoanalysis, and specifically to show that his position on Freudian theory would not come as a surprise to readers familiar with the body of his philosophy, even if they were entirely unaware of his interest in psychoanalysis and his pronouncements on it.

Freud remarks that when psychoanalysis became a subject of discussion in France, Pierre Janet behaved rather badly: "I confess," Freud says, "that for a long time I was willing to accord Janet a very high recognition for his explanation of neurotic symptoms, because he regarded them as expressions of *'idées inconscientes'* possessing the patient's mind. Since then, however, Janet has taken up an attitude of undue reserve, as if he meant to imply that the Unconscious had been nothing more to him than a manner of speaking, a makeshift, *'une façon de parler,'* and that he had nothing 'real' in mind. Since then I have not understood Janet's views, but I believe that he has gratuitously deprived himself of great credit."[3] I have often wondered how Wittgenstein could possibly be so admired by Freudian loyalists when he, too, for reasons of his own, regarded the "hypothesis" of the unconscious as really no more than a manner of speaking which creates more philosophical difficulties than the scientific ones it claims to resolve. It is easy to imagine what Freud's response would have been to a philosopher who maintains that the inventor of psychoanalysis did not "discover" a new field and create the science to go with it, but simply proposed a new determination or extension of the concept: "Extension of a concept in a *theory* (e.g., wish-fulfillment dream)" (*Zettel*, sec. 449). What Wittgenstein refuses to acknowledge in psychoanalysis, as in set theory, is nothing less than its ontology.

While Wittgenstein apparently accepts everything in the new science except, precisely, its central concept of the unconscious, some nonetheless suggest that he may well have played a positive, even seminal, role as an indispensable intermediary in the process that led from Freud to Lacan— that is, from the early Freud to the true Freud. Personally, this strikes me as yet another symptom of the tendency toward wishful thinking (in this case on theoretical and philosophical matters) which psychoanalysts are paid to understand. France has certainly compensated Freud beyond what he could reasonably have hoped, and even beyond anything reasonable, for the disappointment he expresses in the passage on Janet; in any case we French are well known for our tendency to sometimes confuse the practice of philosophy with the practice of free association, and for our sovereign contempt for what Wittgenstein considered more important than anything else in philosophy, namely the recognition of differences. In a conversation with M. O'C. Drury in 1948, after remarking that Berkeley and Kant seemed to him to be profound thinkers, he answers a question concerning Hegel: "Hegel always seems to want to say that things that look different are in reality the same. Whereas what interests me is to show that things that look the same are in reality different." This idea is certainly not very attractive to those who consider the respect for differences, beginning with those which characterize ways of thinking and philosophical styles, to be the mark of impotence or philosophical cowardice, and who find it more convenient to think that what a philosopher like Wittgenstein deliberately refuses to do for philosophical reasons is something he is simply incapable of doing and must be done by others. Surely this explains why his writings have so little effect, in a general way, on the conception and practice of philosophy on the part of people who in principle appeal to his authority. And perhaps this also explains why we have clearly entered into the era of books and articles typically entitled "Wittgenstein and X," in which you can be sure that X is quite deliberately the most unlikely choice. I hasten to add, however, that I do not intend to linger over this aspect of the problem in the present work, which is devoted to what Wittgenstein says about psychoanalysis and not to whether psychoanalysis might succeed in accommodating itself to his remarks without renouncing its central concepts, or even, as is sometimes suggested, in utilizing this kind of criticism, which is generally considered much more "constructive" than Karl Popper's, to try and clarify or ameliorate its position.

While I am convinced that Wittgenstein's remarks indeed mean what they seem to say--namely, that psychoanalysis hasn't much to do with the kind of science it claims to be--I would not like to give the impression of trying to use them chiefly as ammunition for yet another criticism of psychoanalysis. I certainly do not think the question of psychoanalysis can be settled by what Wittgenstein has to say about it, as pertinent as his observations and criticisms in general may be. It is surely difficult, after reading Freud, to maintain that the unconscious might be reduced in the end merely to a simple "form of representation." But it is unfortunately still more difficult to claim that we are now in possession of a coherent and scientifically irreproachable, or even simply acceptable, concept of the unconscious that satisfies the conditions required by Freudian theory. Despite the Copernican revolution Freud is said to have wrought, and all that psychoanalysis is supposed to have "demonstrated" once and for all with regard to the unconscious, the philosopher (whose problem, if we are to believe Wittgenstein, is to restrain his impulse to say more than he knows) must admit that we still do not know whether what Freud says is really intelligible, let alone true.

In a letter from 1945, Wittgenstein wrote to Norman Malcolm, who had begun to read Freud:

> I , too, was greatly impressed when I first read Freud. He's extraordinary.—Of course, he is full of fishy thinking & his charm & the charm of his subject is so great that you may be easily fooled. He always stresses what great forces in the mind, what strong prejudices work against the idea of psycho-analysis. But he never says what an enormous charm that idea has for people, just as it has for Freud himself. There may be strong prejudices against uncovering something nasty, but sometimes it is infinitely more *attractive* than it is repulsive. Unless you think *very* clearly, psycho-analysis is a dangerous & foul practice, & it's done no end of harm & comparatively little good. (If you think I'm being an old spinster—think again!)—All this, of course, doesn't detract from Freud's extraordinary scientific achievement. Only, extraordinary scientific achievements have a way these days of being used for the destruction of human beings (I mean, their bodies, or their souls, *or their intelligence*). *So hold on to your brains.*

It is rather surprising to see Wittgenstein evoke here what he calls "*Freud's extraordinary scientific achievement,*" since his remarks on Freudian theory generally tend to emphasize how far removed it is from science and how close to mythology. We must no doubt conclude that, like many other critics of Freud (Karl Kraus, for example) who were disturbed by the way psychoanalysis had begun to conquer the world, Wittgenstein, too, hesitated over whether the real problem with psychoanalysis was psychoanalysis itself or rather how it was used and will probably continue to be used in an age like ours. Wittgenstein seems to allow that a good use of Freudian theory might exist, but he considers it already amply demonstrated by experience that the requisite conditions, concerning both the state of mind and capacities of the patient as well as the aptitudes of the analyst, can be fulfilled only under very exceptional circumstances. But clearly a scientific instrument that is generally used for perverse and pernicious purposes cannot be criticized in the same way as a mythological construction, which would have in its favor (and, from the philosophical point of view, against it) only its enormous seductive power over weak minds, or at least over those who cannot or would not think clearly. Wittgenstein believes that we have an imperative need for philosophical clarity to save us from the misdeeds of psychoanalysis, yet at least in

France it was thought that philosophy was in greater need of psychoanalytic "science" than psychoanalysis was of philosophical clarification. And indeed this is just what we might expect if Wittgenstein is right.

Wittgenstein did not necessarily condemn as a sin against intelligence the acceptance of a theory that has the enormous advantage of being particularly seductive. But he certainly considered it the basic duty of intelligence (and clearly the duty of philosophy) to try and determine as accurately as possible the exact measure of instinctive and irrational attraction or repulsion involved in our acceptance or refusal of any theory. This was the kind of thing he thought it was essential to *know*, even if there was no guarantee it would lead to a radical modification of our attitude toward the theory in question; and this is precisely the meaning of the philosophic work he himself did on the exemplary case of psychoanalysis. What psychoanalysis teaches us about ourselves may not be primarily, or uniquely, what it thinks: it confronts us, perhaps above all, with the anthropologically and epistemologically significant but perhaps irreducible fact that explanations such as its own are likely to be instantly, almost irresistibly, accepted by people like us. Freud suggests that there are elements in our constitution that make us particularly refractory to the acceptance and practice of psychoanalysis. Wittgenstein maintains that Freud chose to see only one side of the question, and not necessarily the most important. The fascination psychoanalytic explanations hold for the mind of our contemporaries surely reveals something much more interesting and unexpected about the peculiarities of our constitution than our sometimes instinctive refusal to accept the affront to our dignity which the discovery of an intolerable objective truth might represent.

Wittgenstein Reads Freud

CHAPTER I

Wittgenstein:
Disciple of Freud?

Psychoanalysis . . . looks to me not like the science of a
generation but its sole remaining passion.

—KARL KRAUS, "Unauthorized Psychology" (1913)

IT WOULD BE futile to search the work of Wittgenstein for a thorough
discussion or systematic critique of psychoanalysis. Freud's theory is not
the focus of any carefully argued statement, and the materials available to
us on this subject are rather contained in conversations reported by Rush
Rhees and in what are often brief, allusive remarks scattered throughout
Wittgenstein's published writings and manuscripts. Psychoanalysis most
often serves as an illustration in the context of much broader philosophical
discussions concerning questions such as the distinction between reasons
and causes, "aesthetic" explanation and causal explanation, the nature of
symbolism in general, of language, mythology, metaphysics, and the sciences. And the case of Freud is sometimes compared to that of authors like
Darwin and Frazer, whose theories, in Wittgenstein's view, raise some of
the same kinds of perplexities and problems.

Wittgenstein told Rhees that just when he had become convinced psychology was simply a "waste of time," he read Freud and experienced
what he felt was a true revelation. "And for the rest of his life," notes
Rhees, "Freud was one of the few authors he thought worth reading. He
would eagerly speak of himself—at the period of these discussions—as a
'disciple of Freud,' or as a follower of Freud.'"[1] According to Rhees's reck-
oning, Wittgenstein must have read Freud shortly after 1919, yet even as
late as the 1940s he claimed to be a partisan; this did not stop him, however, from formulating extremely negative judgments on psychoanalysis:
"Freud's fanciful pseudo-explanations (precisely because they are brilliant [*geistreich*]) perform a disservice. (Now any ass has these pictures
available to use in 'explaining' symptoms of illness.)"[2] This is hardly the
kind of talk we would expect from an ordinary "disciple." That Wittgen-

stein might have considered psychoanalysis both important and mistaken is at first difficult to understand. Yet this is the same attitude he displayed toward philosophical theories he criticized (beginning with the theory he himself had developed in the *Tractatus*).

Wittgenstein's readings of Freud seem concerned chiefly with the works published before the First World War. The two works he cites most frequently are *The Psychopathology of Everyday Life* and, in particular, *The Interpretation of Dreams*; on several occasions he also alludes to *Jokes and Their Relation to the Unconscious*. But as Brian McGuinness notes,[3] he was probably familiar with much more of Freud's work simply through osmosis. Breuer and Freud's *Studies on Hysteria* figured in the Wittgenstein family library; and passages in which Wittgenstein compares his own position to Freud's in relation to Breuer strongly suggest that he was familiar with its contents. In a remark dated 1939–1940, he observes:

> I believe that my originality (if that is the right word) is an originality belonging to the soil rather than to the seed. (Perhaps I have no seed of my own.) Sow a seed in my soil and it will grow differently than it would in any other soil. Freud's originality too was like this, I think. I have always believed—without knowing why—that the real germ of psychoanalysis came from Breuer, not Freud. Of course Breuer's seed-grain can only have been quite tiny. *Courage* is always original. (*Culture and Value*, p. 36)

In 1948 Wittgenstein told Drury: "Freud's work died with him. No one today can do psychoanalysis in the way he did. Now a book that really would interest me would be the one he wrote in collaboration with Breuer."[4]

Interestingly, in the 1930 remark in which he presents himself as a uniquely "reproductive" thinker who never invented an intellectual movement, Wittgenstein provides a list of authors who inspired and influenced his "work of clarification"; this list includes Boltzmann, Hertz, Schopenhauer, Frege, Russell, Kraus, Loos, Weininger, Spengler, Sraffa, but not Freud (*Culture and Value*, p. 19). At first glance, then, it seems unlikely that the work of Freud can be considered a major influence on Wittgenstein's thought. If he occasionally used Freudian theory as a starting point in his enterprise of clarification, we have no evidence that he felt a serious engagement with psychoanalysis was particularly meaningful or urgent to his own project. The already inordinate importance that psychoanalysis was coming to assume in contemporary culture clearly did not impress him as proof of its philosophical importance.

As Stephen Hilmy notes, there is surely nothing to please a spiritualist in Wittgenstein's remarks on our use of words like "soul" or "mind."[5] For him words are instruments, and in this case, as in any other, the task is simply to describe their function in an accurate fashion. Nor do I believe there is much more to please a follower of psychoanalysis in the positive remarks he happens to make on Freudian theory. But from the moment it became fashionable in France, there was a tendency to think that the most important aspect of Wittgenstein's work must lie in his remarks on "important" things, on aesthetic knowledge, literature, psychoanalysis, religion, and the like, and certainly not in his discussion of the philosophical problems that were really his central preoccupations, and to which he devoted most of his thought. Wittgenstein wanted the *Philosophical Investigations* to be forgotten as soon as possible by "philosophical journalists" and preserved, perhaps, for "a better sort of reader" (cf. *Culture and Value*, p. 66). Unfortunately, given the present circumstances, his work is now likely to be forgotten by better readers, never mind philosophical journalists, before it is really known.

In a note in his journals dated 1936, Drury speaks of a letter from Wittgenstein in which "He suggested that if he did qualify as a doctor, he and I might practice together as psychiatrists" ("Conversations with Wittgenstein," p. 151).

On the limits (and dangers) of psychoanalysis, Wittgenstein expressed himself in the following fashion in a remark made in 1939: "In a way, having oneself psychoanalyzed is like eating from the tree of knowledge. Knowledge acquired sets us (new) ethical problems; but contributes nothing to their solution" (*Culture and Value*, p. 34). It is not surprising that the idea of disclosing his innermost thoughts and motivations to a "soul doctor" provoked such characteristic repugnance. This perfectly conforms to what McGuinness considers to be an essential feature of Wittgenstein's attitude in life, in philosophy, in ethics, and in aesthetics: an extreme restraint and reserve that were utterly opposed to all forms of exhibitionism and explain his deliberate renunciation of theory in philosophy (the difficult thing in philosophy is not to produce theories—we do that quite naturally—but to resist the temptation to do so), as well as his aversion to rhetoric in literature and his dislike of excessive emphasis in musical interpretation. Moreover, Wittgenstein largely shared Karl Kraus's mistrust of the claims of soul medicine in general. When Drury confessed to Wittgenstein that he found the symptoms observed in certain of his patients extremely difficult to understand and in many cases didn't know what to tell them, Wittgenstein remarked: "You must always be puzzled by mental illness. The thing I would dread most, if I became mentally ill, would be your adopting a commonsense attitude; that you could take it for granted that I was deluded. I sometimes wonder whether you will have the right sense of humor for this work. You are too easily shocked when things don't go according to plan" (Drury, "Conversations with Wittgenstein," p. 166). Wittgenstein wondered if the concept of illness itself was really appropriate. In a remark made in 1946, he writes: "Madness need not be regarded as an illness. Why shouldn't it be seen as a sudden—more or *less* sudden—change of character?" (*Culture and Value*, p. 54). He even thought there might be some urgency in changing our view of madness: " 'It is high time for us to compare these phenomena with something *different*'—one might say,—I am thinking, e.g., of mental illnesses" (ibid., p. 55).

Wittgenstein surely had a very concrete experience of psychoanalysis and its possible results—for good or ill. As McGuinness notes ("Freud and Wittgenstein," pp. 28–29), he had lived for quite some time in Vienna or its environs, from the end of the First World War until the year of his return to Cambridge, and had many friends and relations who were impelled to seek psychoanalysis in an attempt to resolve their personal problems. We know that in 1926, just when he had to decide whether to give up the teaching profession, he was obliged to undergo a psychiatric examination. We can imagine how he must have resented what he perceived to be an inadmissible and "alien" intrusion into his private life and personality. Yet he belonged to a milieu (the enlightened upper bourgeoisie) in which Freudian discoveries and revelations (unflattering as they might at first have seemed) provoked considerable curiosity and interest. His sister Margarete maintained personal relations with Freud and had been analyzed by him for reasons that McGuinness tells us amounted largely to "speculative curiosity." Freud sent her a copy of *The Future of an Illusion* dated the day of his departure for England (3 June 1938). She and Wittgenstein liked to tell each other their dreams and to play the exciting game of interpretation. Given his background and the setting in which he grew up, the question is surely not how Wittgenstein came to be interested in Freud's work but rather how he could have avoided it. It can be fairly said that his Viennese origins and his social and family background made him particularly well situated to know that alongside the indignant protests and fierce opposition Freud emphasizes, psychoanalysis managed to elicit infatuations and enthusiasms that were in no way professional, that were in fact somewhat suspect and, from a scientific point of view, rather disreputable.

It was in the same spirit of essentially speculative curiosity that Wittgenstein and his sister—at very different times and to very different ends—both underwent sessions to induce hypnotic trance. According to David Pinsent's account in his journals, in 1913 Wittgenstein, claiming that people in a hypnotic state were capable of extraordinary muscular efforts, wondered if they might also be capable of similar mental efforts and had himself hypnotized twice, requesting the practitioner (a certain Dr. Rogers) to ask him questions on particularly difficult issues of logic which he had not yet solved. The attempt was a complete failure. Dr. Rogers managed to put Wittgenstein to sleep only the second time, but so deeply that it took him half an hour to get fully awake. Wittgenstein declared that he had actually remained conscious during the entire procedure, hearing what was said to him but deprived of any strength of will, incapable of understanding what he was hearing or of making the slightest muscular or intellectual effort.

There is, of course, a considerable distance between curiosity and adherence, a distance Wittgenstein clearly never bridged in the case of psychoanalysis. Strange as it may at first seem, his abiding mistrust of Freudian theory, from the epistemological as well as the ethical point of view, stands in singular contrast to the generally more positive reaction of the members of the Vienna Circle. In an interview Heinrich Neider gave to the journal *Conceptus*, he indicates that, according to his personal recollections, relations between the Vienna Circle and the group attached to Freud "consisted of the fact that, as I have since learned, numerous members of the Vienna Circle were in analysis. Indeed, they had come to Vienna in part because they were going into analysis there. I know that [Rudolf] Carnap—already in the Vienna period and later in America—was in analysis for 20 years. But naturally this was something one didn't talk about."[6] Quite apart from the personal attitude of Carnap and other members of the Circle, it is understandable that for proponents of the "scientific conception of the world" psychoanalysis might at first have seemed to be a rationalist and progressivist enterprise which would eventually, if not immediately, lead a more scientific understanding of mental phenomena, and whose inspiration was flowing in precisely the direction indicated in Carnap's *Der Logische Aufbau der Welt* (1928) and in the manifesto of the Vienna Circle (1929). The least we can say is that Wittgenstein himself was certainly not a proponent of the "scientific conception of the world," had no great expectation that humanity would benefit from the real or supposed conquests of science, and in any case was not at all convinced that psychoanalysis was or could become a science. In a conversation with Rhees in 1942, he contends that "Freud is constantly claiming to be scientific. But what he gives is *speculation*—something prior even to the formation of a hypothesis" (*Lectures and Conversations*, p. 44).

Though we might have feared otherwise, Wittgenstein's reservations with regard to Freudian theory have only rarely been subjected to the kind of psychoanalytic explanations and diagnoses usual in such a case. Nonetheless, in his review of the first volume of McGuinness's biography of Wittgenstein, Stephen Toulmin wonders whether Wittgenstein shouldn't have been psychoanalyzed in his youth, and on this point compares his case with Virginia Woolf's: "He was a few years younger than Virginia Woolf and, like her, belonged to the last of those generations—after the decline of the Confessional, but before the advent of the Couch—who were brought up to assume, and expect of themselves, complete command over their own psychic lives."[7]

Clearly, Toulmin is conscious of the fact that the same education which made Wittgenstein so exacting and merciless toward himself also nourished the development of his extraordinary intellectual gifts. But he still judges that "wise counsel might have helped him, as an adult, to distinguish the constructive demands that he placed on his own creative activities from the unrealistic perfectionism that had destructive effects, both on his capacity to deal happily with people who did not wholly share his attitudes, and on his ability to achieve tranquillity in his own inner life" ("The Unappeased Skeptic," p. 948). This is a facile and not entirely plausible supposition. But if we are to believe Fania Pascal, who taught Wittgenstein Russian when he was thinking of settling in the Soviet Union, "though showing signs of great strains and stresses which he must have undergone in childhood, Wittgenstein in the 1930's was the least neurotic of men."[8] According to her, "He never questioned his motives. . . . He was not inhibited in his relations with other people, provided these people were of his choice and his relations with them on his terms. It would be absurd to call him a perfectionist in the neurotic sense of the word" ("Ludwig Wittgenstein"). Fania Pascal suggests that "we can understand his cavalier attitude towards Freud [as it emerges in his discussions with Rush Rhees and others] once we realize that he himself felt he had no need of Freud" (ibid.). To say, as Fania Pascal does, that he had no perceptible split between ego and superego, for that matter no split of any kind, may well seem quite naive to a professional psychoanalyst. But it is probably best to exercise prudence and abstain from speculating on the eventual benefits Wittgenstein might have derived from a spell on the analyst's couch, had he been disposed to seek clarification and relief in this direction.

While Wittgenstein was never tormented by the problem of his personal relations with psychoanalysis, several episodes indicate nonetheless that the problem of possible relations between the "therapeutic" method he was using in philosophy and psychoanalytic technique did indeed preoccupy him, if only because of the characteristic misunderstanding to which it could, and indeed did, give rise. Malcolm reports Wittgenstein's anger at a popularizing article published by a philosopher in the winter of 1946, in which it was suggested that in Wittgenstein's conception and practice philosophy was becoming a kind of psychoanalysis.[9] Malcolm twice heard him openly reject this assimilation based, in his view, on a characteristic confusion, which prompted him to remark that "they are different techniques." Bouwsma notes a conversation in the course of which the question was raised by Wittgenstein as a typical example of the way philosophic discourse and the teaching of philosophy can be reductive and pernicious: "W. had himself talked about philosophy as in certain ways like psychoanalysis, but in the same way in which he might say that it was like a hundred other things. When he became a professor at Cambridge he submitted a typescript to the committee. Keynes was a member of that committee. Of 140 pages, 72 were devoted to the idea that philosophy is like psychoanalysis. A month later Keynes met him and said that he was much impressed with the idea that philosophy is psychoanalysis. And so it goes."[10]

In the same conversation Wittgenstein compared, as he had done on other occasions, the "incalculable harm" Freud had done to the harm he himself had probably done in philosophy. Apparently he judged that his enterprise could be compared on at least one point with Freud's: both represented the same sort of danger to the public. No doubt Wittgenstein could easily imagine a moment when some malicious (or astute) person would be tempted to say: "Wittgenstein's therapeutic method performs a disservice. Now any ass can claim to treat supposed philosophic maladies." Clearly, something he dreaded above all for the future of his work was the process of mechanization, of trivialization and vulgarization that had already had such disastrous results in the case of psychoanalysis. As we have seen, he did not believe that Freud had, or even might have, true disciples; and he wondered if in his own case he should perhaps fear having them more than he should fear being utterly forgotten.

Even if he sometimes presented himself as a disciple of Freud, Wittgenstein never mentions this notion where we would most expect, namely in his remarks on the philosophy of psychology. And when he alludes to the difference between conscious and unconscious mental states, it is not in a specifically Freudian way but rather to indicate that the distinction between the conscious and the unconscious would constitute an additional source of confusion rather than a real solution to the philosophic problem he is trying to resolve. Not surprisingly, even when philosophy takes psychology as its subject, it seems to be the opposite of a depth philosophy: his view of what characterizes the philosophic method is precisely the fact that there is nothing "hidden" to exhume, that everything is in principle immediately accessible to the surface, and that we already know, in a way, everything we need to know. Certainly his philosophical conception of the nature of psychic phenomena does not mark Wittgenstein as a disciple of Freud.

McGuinness concludes his piece on Freud and Wittgenstein by suggesting that the reasons for the comparison, introduced by Wittgenstein himself (and here, too, it is important to note that this is nothing more than an analogy), must really be sought in quite another direction:

So Wittgenstein wants to avoid the mythology implicit in our first reflections on language. He wants to substitute a form of reflection which avoids it—though perhaps at the risk of introducing a new mythology of its own, that of "use" as something present all at once, for example. He wants to see through the surface of grammar. This (it seems to me) is what made it natural for him to call himself a pupil or follower of Freud, for he had in Freud an example of how a new and deeper but often less flattering interpretation could be substituted for the apparent meaning and at the same time of how a mythology could captivate. He accepted and rejected Freud in equal measure, perhaps healthily. (McGuinness, "Freud and Wittgenstein," pp. 42, 43).

As irritating as Wittgenstein may have found the reduction of philosophy to a form of psychoanalysis, we must admit it may have seemed justified by some of his remarks on the nature of philosophy and philosophic work. He explicitly compares philosophy with a kind of self-analysis that must triumph over certain specific resistances: "Working in philosophy— like work in architecture in many respects—is really more working on oneself. On one's own interpretation. On one's way of seeing things. (And what one expects of them.)" (*Culture and Value*, p. 16). And this work on oneself is essentially work *against* oneself. As Wittgenstein says in one of his manuscripts: "Philosophy is an instrument that is useful only against philosophers and against the philosopher in us." Philosophy demands an effort of the self because it implies a renunciation, which Wittgenstein describes as not a renunciation of the intellect but a renunciation of the will or the emotions. We are renouncing nothing of importance by renouncing certain ways of expressing ourselves that have no useful meaning; "but it can be as difficult as holding back tears or containing an explosion of anger."[11] If we accept the idea that what is demanded of the philosopher is first and foremost a reaction against his natural tendencies and inclinations (never mind that these may be, in the event, merely cultural in origin), we will not be surprised to see Wittgenstein allude to Freud in a rather unexpected place:

> The mathematician is bound to be horrified by my mathematical comments, since he has always been trained to avoid indulging in thoughts and doubts of the kind I develop. He has learned to regard them as something contemptible and, to use an analogy borrowed from psycho-analysis [this passage is reminiscent of Freud], he has acquired a revulsion from them as infantile. That is to say, I trot out all the problems that a child learning arithmetic, etc., finds difficult, the problems that education represses without solving. I say to those repressed doubts: you are quite correct, go on asking, and demand clarification! (*Philosophical Grammar*, pp. 381–82)

In the "Big Typescript," Wittgenstein observes that "the philosopher gives us the word with which the thing can be expressed and made inoffensive" (p. 180). This is almost word for word how Breuer and Freud describe what they are doing in *Studies on Hysteria*. The disappearance of hysterical symptoms occurs when the process at the source of the troubles can be reproduced and "expressed" (*ausgesprochen*); more precisely, when the patient has become capable of giving a detailed account of the process and giving voice to the accompanying affect.[12] Further on Wittgenstein emphasizes that, as in the case of psychoanalysis, philosophical therapy can work only on the condition that the patient acknowledges the philosopher's description as the correct expression of his disturbed state: "It is only when he acknowledges it [psychoanalysis] as such as its correct expression ("Big Typescript"). We can locate two other important analogies. The first suggests that, like the therapeutic practice of the psychoanalyst, the practice of the philosopher aims as much as possible at identifying and eliminating the causes of the trouble, and not simply making the symptoms disappear by somehow preventing "pathogenic" ideas from being expressed.[13] The second is that in the practice of both psychoanalysis and philosophy, it is impossible to proceed directly by promptly proposing to the patient the diagnosis likely to reveal the source of his difficulties. As Freud says: " *It is quite hopeless to try to penetrate directly to the nucleus of the pathogenic organization.* Even if we ourselves could guess it, the patient would not know what to do with the explanation offered to him and he would not be psychologically changed by it" (Freud, "Psychotherapy of Hysteria," in *Studies on Hysteria*, p. 292). In the same way, as Wittgenstein emphasizes, "one must not in philosophy attempt to short-circuit problems" (*Wittgenstein's Lectures, Cambridge 1932–1935*, p. 109). The only way is to attack the problem from the periphery—that is, to begin by allowing the patient spontaneously to express his or her philosophical nonsense.

In a conversation with Bouwsma in 1949, Wittgenstein declared that "all his years of teaching had done more bad than good. And he compared it to Freud's teachings. The teachings, like wine, had made people drunk. They did not know how to use the teaching soberly. Did I understand? Oh yes, they had found a formula. Exactly." (*Conversations, 1949–1951*, pp. 11–12.) Wittgenstein told Rhees that he would have to resign himself to seeing psychoanalysis exercise a considerable and pernicious influence for some time to come: "It will take a long time before we lose our subservience to it" (*Lectures and Conversations*, p. 41). To learn something about Freud, he observes, a critical attitude is essential; and (as the entire history of the psychoanalytic movement and psychoanalytic culture retrospectively confirms) theories like Freud's have the inconvenience, among others, of eliciting forms of allegiance that make criticism particularly difficult, if not impossible. It is significant that Wittgenstein thought a critical and, as he says, "sober" use of his own teachings might well be nearly as difficult and unlikely. In a way, although he certainly had no doubt about the intrinsic importance of his philosophic work, he was convinced that it had every chance of being, in the short run and perhaps for some time, as noxious as Freud's.

Freud considered it indispensable to create a school around himself to spread his ideas and increasingly impose the revolutionary truths he was convinced he had discovered. Wittgenstein did not believe that philosophy had new truths to communicate and did not want to create a school. In 1947 he said that he was not sure he "preferred a continuation of my work by others to a change in the way people live that would make all these questions superfluous" (*Culture and Value*, p. 61). His worry and apprehension over the effects of his teaching and the kind of posterity it might create would prompt him to compare his case rather with Breuer than with Freud. It was said of Breuer that in a way he had been prevented from completely exploiting his revolutionary discoveries by excessive scientific caution and a certain consciousness of the potential dangers inherent in the utilization of the new techniques he had helped to refine. There is indeed a singular contrast between Breuer's tendency to minimize his personal originality and downplay the importance of his own contributions, his mistrust of excessive generalizations and his tendency to abstain systematically from any definitive conclusion, and Freud's unshakable self-assurance, his impressive boldness, his relative absence of scruples, and his predilection for universal and extravagant generalizations.

Breuer's humility before both the facts and the explanations of others emerges clearly in the conclusion of his theoretical contribution to the volume composed in collaboration with Freud. He states:

> The attempt . . . to make a synthetic construction of hysteria out of what we know of it today is open to the reproach of eclecticism, if such a reproach can be justified at all. There were so many formulations of hysteria, from the old "reflex theory" to the "dissociation of personality," which have had to find a place in it. But it can scarcely be otherwise, for so many excellent observers and acute minds have concerned themselves with hysteria. It is unlikely that any of their formulations was without a portion of the truth. A future exposition of the true state of affairs will certainly include them all and will merely combine all the one-sided views of the subject into a corporate reality. Eclecticism, therefore, seems to me nothing to be ashamed of. (Breuer, "Theoretical" in *Studies on Hysteria*, p. 295)

Breuer ends his essay by observing that the best data available on hysteria may not represent much more than a vague play of shadows, but that we can reasonably hope "there may be some degree of correspondence and similarity between the real processes and our idea of them" (ibid.).

From the outset Freud's behavior was clearly quite different. He was generally convinced that there had to be *one* correct explanation and quickly persuaded himself that he had found, or in any case could find, it.

Both by temperament and because he thought this should be the normal position of philosophy on all questions of this kind, Wittgenstein's attitude was much closer to Breuer's "unproductive" skepticism than to Freud's creative dogmatism. As we shall see, he considered Freud's approach to be much more philosophical (in the pejorative sense) than scientific. If we recall that Wittgenstein believed all philosophical difficulties originated in a conviction that "*It must* be this way (although it may not be this way)" and in the desire to preserve at any cost a seductive paradigm or mode of description, it is not difficult to understand what he found questionable (philosophically and a fortiori scientifically) in Freud's method. For Wittgenstein, a person who thinks there must be *one correct* explanation and *one correct* reason for the sort of phenomena treated by psychoanalysis is not someone who is simply adopting the dominant scientific attitude but someone who is already on the road to producing a mythology.

Breuer thought that in addition to his characteristic predilection for absolute and exclusive formulations, Freud may have been moved by a certain desire to "épater le bourgeois," or shock people (and indeed he succeeded in this, even if the shock was not as great as he had hoped or feared). This explanation is probably a little simplistic. But what is certainly typical of Freud's approach is the way he managed to create and sustain the myth of the heroic scientist who imposes revolutionary discoveries by conquering formidable prejudice,[14] an attitude usually coupled with the tendency to consider that the simple fact of challenging a prejudice already implies a powerful presumption of truth, or even justifies a personal claim to possess the truth. Wittgenstein was clearly not impressed by this kind of mythology, to which he seems to have been in general particularly impervious (his model of real intellectual courage was Gottlob Frege rather then Freud). Georg Cantor also offered himself, and has frequently been offered (with more reason), as the prototype of the revolutionary scientist who collided with a conspiracy of prejudice and was the victim, under the circumstances, of a reactionary and obtuse mathematical community. Wittgenstein was not tempted, to say the least, to consider Cantor's difficulties as an argument in favor of the theory of transfinite sets. Gödel's case was obviously quite different, since the opposition he foresaw and dreaded did not really manifest itself or was almost immediately disarmed. But there is at least one constant in the way Wittgenstein reacted to each of these situations. He was not really convinced that the philosophical importance of these three scientific revolutions (real or supposed) was as considerable as is generally assumed, or that this importance lies where we might expect. We could say that in all three cases he was looking for a kind of austere comprehension that would imply no concession to something he particularly despised and considered a sickness of the times, namely scientific sensationalism, the utterly dishonest exploitation—so he thought—of the greater public's superficial curiosity about the latest discoveries of science. Unfortunately, authentically revolutionary scientists can easily count on the superficiality and incomprehension of philosophers to help them when they are ready to surrender to this kind of temptation.

It is quite possible that there was a certain ambivalence in Wittgenstein's reaction to the almost total lack of inhibition so characteristic of Freud's intellectual approach, and in general to the founder of psychoanalysis. His opinion of Freud is condensed in a striking and illuminating way in the following remark: "Freud has very intelligent reasons for saying what he says, a great imagination and colossal prejudice, and prejudice which is very likely to mislead people" (*Lectures and Conversations*, p. 26). Wittgenstein admired Freud for his intelligence, his imagination, his inventiveness, and his ingenuity. But while appreciating such qualities in a thinker, he always regarded them with a certain suspicion, and in his own case as well. Rhees reports that once when Wittgenstein was recounting something Freud had said and the advice he had given someone, one of those present remarked that this advice did not seem very wise; to which Wittgenstein responded: "Oh certainly not. But wisdom is something I never would expect from Freud. Cleverness, certainly; but not wisdom" (*Lectures and Conversations*, p. 41). I confess I don't really understand what prompted Paul-Laurent Assoun to declare that "this was a position borrowed from the man who played the role of Wittgenstein's father confessor, Ludwig Hansel,"[15] and which seemed to be a reaction of Catholic puritanism. It may be that on this point, as on a number of others, Wittgenstein was indeed influenced by Hansel, who was a deeply believing Catholic and reproached psychoanalysis for its misunderstanding of moral and religious questions; but it is unlikely that when he accuses Freud of lacking wisdom, or even when he accuses him of being irreligious, Wittgenstein is basically expressing a puritanical opinion on the dangers psychoanalysis could pose for conventional morality and religion (in this case the Catholic religion, if I understand correctly). Assoun reminds us that "Wittgenstein, originally a Jew, was baptized in the Catholic faith, thought of becoming a monk and had a Catholic funeral" (*Freud et Wittgenstein*, p. 49). He evidently forgets that, as McGuinness quite rightly says, "He [Wittgenstein] felt more sympathy than faith"[16] for religion in general and Catholicism in particular, that despite the Wittgenstein family's nominal Catholicism, their style of life on the whole was rather Protestant, that Wittgenstein himself never explicitly followed any religious practice, and that the question whether he should or shouldn't be given a religious burial posed a real problem of conscience for his friends. In 1929 Wittgenstein told Drury: "Make sure that your religion is a matter between you and God only" ("Conversations with Wittgenstein," p. 117), and some time later: "For all you and I can tell, the religion of the future will do without any priests or ministers. I think one of the things you and I have to learn is that we have to live without the consolation of belonging to a church" (ibid., p. 129). He also told Drury he was convinced that all religious organizations were more or less equally worthy, and not very worthy at that. He especially detested all forms of theoretical and philosophical discourse on things like morality and religion, whether by traditional organizations or by the free thinkers who opposed them in the name of reason. Drury confesses that he was surprised to hear Wittgenstein declare in 1929: "Russell and the clergy have together done infinite harm, infinite harm" ("Conversations with Wittgenstein," p. 117). If we want to understand the meaning of the remark cited by Rhees, we might do better to ask ourselves, as Rhees suggests, why Wittgenstein found in the narratives of Gottfried Keller (in particular, *Green Heinrich*) the kind of wisdom he found lacking in Freud; and to ponder why, when he willingly practiced the examination of conscience and confession (several of his friends recall the "confessions" he felt the need to make at certain moments), it apparently wouldn't have occurred to him to consult a psychoanalyst to increase his chances of achieving what he considered the supreme good, in philosophy as well as life--namely, utter clarity and complete honesty in one's relations with oneself.

McGuinness notes that "the character of Heinrich Lee in *Green Heinrich* . . . is also very reminiscent of Ludwig and his judgments of himself, both in his shame about the betrayals of youth and his sense (justified in Heinrich's case) that he had constantly refused and withdrawn when an opportunity was given him."[17] On the other hand, it seems that the desire to imitate the example of Keller (whose journals he had read) played a certain role in his keeping a journal at various times over the years, in which he copied down the thoughts that came to mind about himself and his own life (cf. *Wittgenstein: A Life* 1:56). The interesting question is why he clearly preferred this "naive" form of self-analysis, or that of the hero in Keller's bildungsroman, to the much harsher but in his view not necessarily more profitable "scientific" insights offered by psychoanalysis. Obsessed as he was to the end of his life by the problem of his inadequacies and personal failures, he tended to consider it the better part of wisdom to mistrust the rather too tempting fruit of the psychoanalytic tree of knowledge.

In order to understand Wittgenstein's reticence toward psychoanalysis, we should remember that Freud and his disciples had already provided a few remarkable and well-known examples of what can surely be considered a highly characteristic lack of wisdom in their way of using the methods of the new science of the soul to analyze a number of exemplary "cases" of writers and artists of the past, and even of the immediate present. Kraus himself had been favored with such a treatment in a session on 12 January 1910, an operation that Thomas Szasz characterizes as "Wittel's psychoanalytic character assassination of Kraus"[18] (with at least the passive complicity of Freud); and Kraus had reacted to this procedure by denouncing the obsessional simplifying behavior of the "psychoanal," a murderous pun that flings back in his face the psychoanalyst's tact in dealing with things he doesn't understand. What unleashed Kraus's revolt and completed his break with psychoanalysis seems to have been chiefly the unconsidered and sometimes frankly absurd application of analytic technique to the interpretation of literary and artistic works, and the formulation of pretentious and equally hazardous diagnoses of creators who should have inspired a bit more respect, in his view, if only because the dead cannot pose the slightest resistance to this sort of violent intrusion. In his piece "Unauthorized Psychology" (1913), Kraus asserts that psychoanalysts leave their victims no way out, dead or alive:

> The only thing that I consciously have to fear from psychoanalysis is the unauthorized reproduction of my texts. This much is certain, but who will vouch for my unconscious? I, of course, know nothing about it, only the psychoanalysts do. They know where the trauma lies buried, and they hear the grass growing on a complex. The book-keepers of compulsive actions are everywhere: they have not let Grillparzer, Lenau or Kleist escape them, and as for Goethe's sorcerer's apprentice, they only disagree as to whether it is masturbation or bed wetting that is being sublimated. If I tell them they can kiss my ass, I must have an anal predilection. There is no doubt, say the doubters, that my battle is a rebellion against the father, and the incest motif lurks between my lines. Appearances are against me. It would be wasted effort to try and prove that libido isn't involved—they have caught me![19]

But if we cannot go so far as to credit Wittgenstein with Kraus's conviction that science in general (including its latest avatar, psychoanalysis) ought to renounce once and for all any attempt to penetrate the mysteries of the soul, it is not difficult to imagine what he might have thought of the explanatory claims psychoanalysis had already clearly displayed with regard to productions of art and literature, and which he was certainly not ready to excuse as simple excess or youthful error. In 1949 he said to Drury: "I have always thought that Darwin was wrong: his theory doesn't account for all this variety of species. It hasn't the necessary multiplicity. Nowadays some people are fond of saying that at last evolution has produced a species that is able to understand the whole process which gave it birth. Now that you can't say" ("Conversations with Wittgenstein," p. 174). He was apparently convinced that when it comes to things like thought and understanding, a theory like evolution hasn't the explanatory means equal to the task. For similar reasons, he must have thought that psychoanalysis lacked the "requisite multiplicity" to explain the higher productions of art and literature when it uses them merely as raw material for psychoanalysis. In this case, too, there is a kind of confusion of "orders" and an immediately palpable difference between the category of the presumed explanation and that of the phenomena it is meant to explain. And the situation is clearly not very different when the *explicandum* is of an ethical or religious nature.

In a sense, then, aside from any question of puritanism, Catholic or Protestant, Wittgenstein suspected Freud of having a poor understanding of morality or religion. Had he read *The Future of an Illusion* he might have reacted as he did to Frazer's explanations of the magical or religious beliefs of primitives, and objected that these things can never be treated as errors or illusions which superior knowledge (in this case "scientific knowledge") reveals as such. Indeed, Freud thought that "comparative research has been struck by the fatal resemblance between the religious ideas we revere and the mental products of primitive peoples and times."[20] But this resemblance can be considered fatal only if one considers the mental products in question more or less as Frazer does. In 1949 Wittgenstein observed: "One can, it is true, compare a belief solidly implanted in us to a superstition, but it may also be said that one must always find oneself again on solid ground, whether it is now an image or something else, and that consequently an image fundamental to all our thought must be respected and not treated as superstition" (*Culture and Value*, p. 83). Thus there are beliefs too fundamental to shake or discredit simply by invoking the fact that they have no serious basis. It may be impossible, for this reason, to treat religions like a collective delirium, an "attempt to procure a certainty of happiness and a protection against suffering through a delusional remoulding of reality."[21]

Because he does not treat religion primarily as a system of representations (whose falseness or delusional character might be demonstrated), and does not believe in the real importance of the reasons and "arguments" advanced in favor of religious doctrines, Wittgenstein judges completely naive the idea that under the influence of scientific thinking humanity as a whole would finally see that these doctrines are entirely inadequate or nonexistent and accept the logical consequences. But on this point Freud is certainly no naive. He himself believed his enterprise was "completely inoffensive" (*Civilization and Its Discontents*, p. 57). "There is," he admits, "no danger of a devout believer's being overcome by my arguments and deprived of his faith" (ibid., pp. 57–58). The crucial point is rather that by proposing a psychological—and psychologistic—explanation of the origin of religious beliefs (which constitutes the "scientific" explanation), Freud is also committing an error typical of the "modernists" (whether believers or free thinkers), who in Wittgenstein's view completely misunderstand the nature (that is, the *function*) of religious symbolism and of symbolism in general.

It is noteworthy, too, that Freud labels a belief "illusory" in which the motive of wish fulfillment triumphs over the desire for a confrontation with the real, obliterating it completely, and along with it any possible confirmation by reality (cf. ibid., p. 56). Yet Wittgenstein does not believe that in the case of religious beliefs there can be any confrontation with reality, more for reasons of "logic" (in Wittgenstein's sense of the word) than psychology. In remarks made in 1947, he writes:

> It strikes me that a religious belief can be only something like a passionate decision in favor of a system of reference. Therefore, although it may be a *belief*, it is all the same a way of life or a way of judging life. An act consistent with passionately seizing upon *this* way of seeing. And the instruction given in a religious belief ought therefore to be the presentation, the description of this system of reference, and at the same time an appeal to conscience. And these two things finally ought to make the instructed person himself, of his own volition, passionately embrace the system of reference in question. This would be as if someone, on the one side, made me see my desperate situation, and, on the other, offered me the means to salvation, when, of my own volition, or in any case without the *instructor* leading me by the hand, I throw myself on it and seize upon it. (*Culture and Value*, p. 64).

We might challenge a theory of religious belief like Freud's by objecting that a system of reference one adopts in order to judge reality cannot be evaluated in terms of its correspondence or lack of correspondence to reality. It may be that the adoption of the system in question actually bears closer resemblance, under the circumstances, to an affair of the heart than to a rational matter. But this is precisely the point of resemblance, in Wittgenstein's view, between the choice of a particular conception of the world and the choice of a religious way of life. If replacing passion with reflection and knowledge involves demanding in advance that the system of reference be *justified* by reality, this demand is impossible for reasons that have nothing to do with what, in the case of adherence to a theory or statement, might be called credulity, blindness, or haste. The impossibility of dispassionately judging something that functions in our thought and life as a system of reference constitutes, we know, one of the central themes of Wittgenstein's philosophy. The attempt to treat this impossibility as an unacceptable deficiency for a rational mind is already proof of a fundamental misunderstanding of the nature of what is involved. Freud might be accused, then, not of overestimating the intellect (not much of a risk in his case), but rather of overestimating the importance and pertinence of a psychological approach and of an inquiry into the psychological "truth" of situations of this kind.

In a celebrated passage from *The Psychopathology of Everyday Life*, Freud has recourse to the analogy of paranoia to explain the irrational character of conceptions of the world that are expressed in mythology, religion, and philosophy itself:

> I believe that a large part of the mythological view of the world, which extends a long way into most modern religions, *is nothing but psychology projected into the external world*. The obscure recognition (the endopsychic perception, as it were) of psychical factors and relations in the unconscious is mirrored—it is difficult to express it in other terms, and here the analogy with paranoia must come to our aid—in the construction of a *supernatural reality*, which is destined to be changed back once more by science into the *psychology of the unconscious*. One could venture to explain in this way the myths of paradise and the fall of man, of God, of good and evil, of immortality, and so on, and to transform *metaphysics* into *metapsychology*.[22]

There is, of course, nothing shocking to Wittgenstein in Freud's comparison of philosophy with things like primitive animism, paranoia, or madness (Wittgenstein himself used or sometimes suggested comparisons of this kind). The problem is rather that he does not believe in the possibility of retranslating metaphysical constructions (whether those of philosophy or those of mythology and religion) into the discourse of a psychological science or a metapsychology, or of any science at all. The science that is supposed to allow this metapsychological retranscription of the paranoid systematizings and speculations of philosophy in terms of oppositions and conflicts originating in the unconscious is, in fact, a new mythology without knowing it. The psychology of the unconscious considered as the theory of a new field opened to scientific inquiry by the psychoanalyst is itself nothing more than a speculative construction of the same kind, one that employs the same procedures as those myths whose true nature and illusory, infantile character it claims to reveal. The therapy of philosophical maladies must therefore renounce once again the consolation of leaning on any scientific foundation. There is no science that accounts for the illusions to which philosophy falls victim, and no scientifically established technique that can free philosophic understanding from the obsessive and false analogies which are at the source of the insoluble problems it confronts; in other words, there is no method more or less comparable in its claims to the psychoanalytic method for transforming latent nonsense into manifest nonsense. In the early 1930s Wittgenstein was convinced he had found a method that would allow him henceforth to treat all philosophic problems with the professionalism and efficacy appropriate to an age like ours. But he certainly did not believe that this method was scientific.

Freud did have the prudence to recognize something his disciples have regularly forgotten since, that: "Psychoanalysis can . . . indicate the subjective and individual motives behind philosophical theories which have ostensibly sprung from impartial logical work, and can draw a critic's attention to the weak spots in the system. It is not the business of psychoanalysis, however, to undertake such criticism itself, for, as may be imagined, the fact that a theory is psychologically determined (*die psychologische Determinierung*) does not in the least invalidate its scientific truth."[23] But the idea of a possible retranscription of metaphysics into metapsychology is obviously far removed from this kind of modesty and benevolent neutrality. The new psychological science is truly considered capable of demonstrating that metaphysical systems as a whole are condemned by their origins to being nothing but chimerical constructs, lacking any objective validity. Freud, too, has in mind an ambitious agenda to eliminate metaphysics in favor of the "scientific" conception of the world. And we know what Wittgenstein thought of the naïveté of all such agendas, and of the idea that the crucial question to be posed with regard to philosophical systems might be whether they are "scientifically correct."

As I have already suggested in speaking of the "ambivalence" of his reactions to Freud, Wittgenstein's reservations with regard to certain aspects of Freud's talent are probably explained in part by the fact that he considered himself gifted with comparable qualities (in particular, the richness of imagination and the talent for inventing and exploiting analogies) and exposed to similar temptations, aptitudes, and risks. He, too, feared being too clever at times, and not profound enough or wise. As he says to Bouwsma: "'Why should I teach? What good will it do for X to listen to me? Only a man who thinks can derive any profit from that sort of thing.' He made an exception for a few students who had a certain obsession and were serious. 'But most of them come to me because I am clever, and I am clever, but this doesn't matter. And they simply want to be clever. . . . The tightrope walker is clever too.'" (*Conversations, 1949–1951*, pp. 9–10). Coming from him, modifiers like "clever" or "*geistreich*," which Wittgenstein used to describe Freud, in fact always implied an element of implicit criticism. Moreover, as McGuinness remarks, "It was a fairly common criticism of himself by Wittgenstein that he was too attached to this quality" ("Freud and Wittgenstein," p. 30). In a letter to Paul Engelmann, dated 1925, we find the following confession: "I know that brilliance (the riches of the spirit [*Geistreichtum*]) is not the ultimate good, and yet I wish now I could die in a moment of brilliance [*in einem geistreichen Augenblick*]."[24] We should probably keep such remarks in mind in trying to understand the nature of Wittgenstein's ethical reproach when he deplores Freud's excessive cleverness and lack of wisdom.

When Wittgenstein qualifies Freud's explanations as "seductive," I do not believe this implies that he personally experienced particular difficulties resisting them or freeing himself from their charms. I do not know to what extent he really includes himself in the "we," when he says that we need time to extricate ourselves from our subservience to them. There is certainly no comparison between the intensity of his lifelong struggle to resolve the philosophical problems that really compelled him and his struggle to explain the ideas of Freud. I consider rather arbitrary, then, or at least quite exaggerated, something like Assoun's version of the case: "Wittgenstein has no illusions when he begins his 'emancipation' from Freudian sovereignty. His criticism simply marks this period of reflection on the causes and modalities of this sovereignty. Indeed, because in his view he cannot help being a 'disciple of Freud' and a 'partisan of Freud,' he must understand the principle of *seduction* that makes this feudal bondage possible—which will perhaps make it possible to undo the hidden effects of this sovereignty" (*Freud et Wittgenstein*, p. 15). We would have to assume just such a Freudian sovereignty, which Wittgenstein himself would have had the greatest difficulty eluding—even in the period of the "Conversations on Freud" (which were not merely conversations)—if we want to justify the sort of confrontation Assoun suggests, and to draw so many conclusions from just a few remarks taken out of context.[25] Without it we run the strong risk of falling once more into the "doxographic" fault of all published studies on the relations between Wittgenstein and Freud, namely that in this kind of work "psychoanalysis functions as a theme of Wittgensteinian criticism, and Freud as an esprit de rencontre" (*Freud et Wittgenstein*, p. 15). Yet at first sight this is indeed how it looks when we turn to Wittgenstein himself. For him Freud was certainly more than simply an intellectual adversary; whether he should be considered a privileged interlocutor and psychoanalysis something more than a theme of Wittgensteinian criticism (among many others, some clearly much more important) is something that, to my mind, remains to be seen.

The Problem of the Reality
of the Unconscious

What, then, . . . can a philosopher say to a theory which, like psycho-analysis, asserts that on the contrary what is mental is in itself *unconscious* and that being conscious is only a *quality* which may or may not accrue to a particular mental act and the withholding of which may perhaps alter that act in no other respect?

—SIGMUND FREUD, "The Resistances to Psycho-Analysis" (1925).

FREUD HAS OFTEN been credited, if not with an actual "discovery" of the unconscious (which he had the wisdom not to claim entirely for himself), at least with the introduction of a revolutionary idea of its nature and function. It is less frequently noticed, however, that his vision of consciousness remained utterly traditional and bound to the idea of consciousness as the internal perception of "objects" of a certain type—the paradigm of clear and immediate perception. Ernest Tugendhat, among others, has rightly insisted on this fact, which is not inconsequential;[1] and indeed Freud's conception of the nature of consciousness conforms perfectly to the classic model. Breuer expresses this when he writes: "We call those ideas conscious which we are aware of. There exists in human beings the strange fact of self-consciousness. We are able to view and observe, as though they were objects, ideas that emerge in us and succeed one another. . . . We describe as conscious those ideas which we observe as active in us, or which we should so observe if we attended to them" (Breuer, "Theoretical," in *Studies on Hysteria*, p. 222). In a frequently cited passage from "The Unconscious" (1915), Freud writes:

> In psycho-analysis there is no choice for us but to declare mental processes to be in themselves unconscious, and to compare the perception of them by consciousness with the perception of the outside world through the sense-organs; we even hope to extract fresh knowledge from the comparison. The

psycho-analytic assumption of unconscious mental activity appears to us, on
one hand, a further development over that of primitive animism which
caused our own consciousness to be reflected all around us, and, on the other
hand, it seems to be an extension of the corrections begun by Kant of our view
in regard to external perception. Just as Kant warned us not to overlook the
fact that our perception is subjectively conditioned and must not be regarded
as identical with the phenomena perceived but never really discerned, so
psycho-analysis bids us not to set the conscious perception in the place of the
unconscious mental process which is its object. The mental, like the physical,
is not necessarily in reality just what it appears to us to be. It is, however,
satisfactory to find that the correction of inner perception does not present
difficulties so great as that of outer perception—that the inner object is less
hard to discern truly than is the outside world.[2]

Against the tendency of philosophers to identify the mental with the
conscious, Freud maintains that the mental should rather be considered
essentially unconscious, and only accidentally and occasionally endowed
with the property we call consciousness; for a mental object, he contends,
the fact of being perceived is nearly as contingent and secondary as it is for
a physical one. And in his view there is nothing problematic in the distinction we make between conscious and unconscious: "[It] is in the last resort
a question of a perception which must be either affirmed or denied, and
the act of perception itself tells us nothing of the reason why a thing is or
is not perceived."[3] But it is clear that if unconscious mental processes were
simply unperceived, in contrast to processes that are perceived, there
would be nothing specifically Freudian in this use of the word "unconscious." A large portion of the mental processes we call "unconscious," in
the sense that they are not present to consciousness at a given moment (but
are not excluded from it in themselves in any permanent way), are not
unconscious in the Freudian sense. Unconscious processes, in the strictly
Freudian sense of the term, are not only processes which the conscious
mind does not perceive at the moment they are taking place, but processes
which it cannot perceive because something is preventing it. These are not
only unknown processes but processes the subject "does not want to
know," and they can succeed in making themselves known only indirectly
and in a disguised form that renders them more or less unrecognizable. As
Freud emphasizes, psychoanalytic theory asserts that "such ideas cannot
become conscious because a certain force is opposed to them, otherwise
they could become conscious and then one would see how little they differ
from other elements which are admittedly mental" (*The Ego and the Id*,
pp. 11–12). In other words, "We obtain our concept of the unconscious,
therefore, from the theory of repression. The repressed serves us as a
prototype of the unconscious" (ibid.). Unconscious processes in this sense,

then, must be such that (1) they are legitimately inferred because the hypothesis of their existence is indispensable to explain perceptible behavioral and mental effects, and (2) their presence can manifest itself only within the limits and in the forms specified by the theory, which do not correspond to what we should perceive if we were not prevented from perceiving them. Psychoanalytic technique—and it alone—can triumph over resistance and bring to consciousness ideas that resistance has previously made inaccessible.

Two important consequences follow from this with regard to Wittgenstein's position on the problem of the unconscious: (1) to the extent that he challenges the model of consciousness as an organ of sensory perception that gives us access to (direct) knowledge of the mental, Wittgenstein cannot fail to find philosophically confused the idea that unconscious phenomena have the particular quality of not being perceived in the sense that conscious phenomena are. In a more general way, unconscious phenomena are not "unknown" in the sense that conscious phenomena might properly speaking be said to be "known." A statement like "I am sick," for example, is not really comparable to a judgment of perception and does not distinguish itself from "He is sick" by effecting an act of direct knowledge, which is replaced in the second case by an inference; (2) if the model itself is inadequate, Freud's crucial distinction between the simply descriptive meaning and the dynamic meaning of the word "unconscious" would be of doubtful use. I have dealt elsewhere and at length with Wittgenstein's criticism of the idea of internal or introspective meaning and the notion that our descriptions of our immediate experience convey facts which we observe in some way in themselves, so I will not go into detail here. I will simply note that such criticism would be devastating, or at least crippling, to the notion that consciousness perceives events taking place in a kind of interior space so that some are perceived, some are not (but might be), and indeed some cannot be because something is preventing it.

One of Freud's favorite metaphors consists of the image of two rooms with a doorkeeper standing between them who exercises control over the ideas that try to go from the first to the second, and decides whether or not to grant them passage. "I should like to assure you," he writes, "that these crude hypotheses, the two chambers, the door-keeper on the threshold between the two, and consciousness as a spectator at the end of the second room, must indicate an extensive approximation to the actual reality."[4] The idea of a sort of locale for storing and maintaining mental objects that may be inaccessible to perception but are nonetheless present in a way that can be felt by effects of quite another kind clearly raises numerous problems, and these have been frequently discussed. But a reader of Wittgen-

stein will probably find just as problematic and questionable the idea of a
locale in which objects are, or may be, subject to the gaze of a witnessing
consciousness. The fact is that when Wittgenstein uses the word "unconscious," he generally does it in an essentially descriptive sense, and even in
his criticism of Freud he gives the impression of curiously neglecting the
properly dynamic aspect, which is so essential. He denounces as a source
of constant confusion the fact that we usually speak of mental states to
designate both conscious states and hypothetical states of an unconscious
mental mechanism. Indeed, the difference is much greater than we are
inclined to believe. The "grammar" of unconscious states and processes is
actually different from that of conscious states or processes. But it is
clearly tempting to regard this as relatively unimportant, and to consider,
as Freud does, that though conscious states are perceived and unconscious
states are not, they may nonetheless have exactly the same properties. As
we shall see, one of the essential problems in Freud's case, as Wittgenstein
sees it, is that he is forced to resort broadly to the grammar of conscious
processes to describe unconscious processes and the functioning of the unconscious mechanism he postulates, while this mechanism obeys laws that
are in principle completely different. To be sure, the mythological aspect
of Freud's thought does not lie in his postulating the existence of an unconscious mental mechanism meant to explain the actions of the mind, or
even in his proposing a concrete model of what this kind of mechanism
might be. Mythology is, as always, generated only by the superficial analogies between things that are, from the grammatical point of view, completely different. As Wittgenstein says, in grammar there are no *small* differences. The difficulty of Freud's position might be summed up, then, in
the two following propositions: (1) the mental is intrinsically unconscious
and consciousness adds nothing essential; (2) however, for reasons that
are equally intrinsic, it can be conceptualized and described only from a
point of view that remains fundamentally that of consciousness: "For it is
easy to describe the unconscious and to follow its developments if it is
approached from the direction of its relation to the conscious, with which
it has so much in common. On the other hand, there still seems no possibility of approaching from the direction of physical events. So that it is bound
to remain a matter for psychological study" ("The Claims of Psycho-Analysis" [1913], p. 179). Kurt Koffka notes:

> When one found it necessary to go beyond consciousness in the description
> and exploration of mind, one imagined the non-conscious parts of mind to be
> fundamentally alike to the conscious one, fundamentally alike, that is, in its
> aspects or properties with the exception of being conscious. Consequently, the
> so-called elements of mind were thought to exist in two forms, the conscious
> and the unconscious.[5]

Despite the revolution Freud is said to have wrought in our way of perceiving and understanding the unconscious, he is no exception to the rule: "Unconscious desire is exactly like conscious desire, except that it is not conscious. This betrays the same predilection; the mind is specifically conscious, consequently all that is mental must be conceived in terms of consciousness, even if it is not itself conscious" (Koffka, "On the Structure of the Unconscious," p. 47).

In his *Lectures, Cambridge 1932–1935*, Wittgenstein devotes a long passage to a discussion of Freud's work which is worth quoting in its entirety:

> I wish to remark on a certain sort of connection which Freud cites, between the fetal position and sleep, which looks to be a causal one but which is not, inasmuch as a psychological experiment cannot be made. His explanation does what aesthetics does: puts two factors together.
>
> Another matter which Freud treats psychologically but whose investigation has the character of an aesthetic one is the nature of jokes. The question, "What is the nature of a joke?" is like the question, "What is the nature of a lyric poem?" I wish to examine in what way Freud's theory is a hypothesis and in what way not. The hypothetical part of his theory, the subconscious, is the part which is not satisfactory. Freud thinks it is part of the essential mechanism of a joke to conceal something, say, a desire to slander someone, and thereby to make it possible for the subconscious to express itself. He says that people who deny the subconscious really cannot cope with post-hypnotic suggestion, or with waking up at an unusual hour of one's own accord. When we laugh without knowing why, Freud claims that by psychoanalysis we can find out. I see a muddle here between a cause and a reason. Being clear why you laugh is not being clear about *a cause*. If it were, then agreement to the analysis given of the joke as explaining why you laugh would not be a means of detecting it. The success of the analysis is supposed to be shown by the person's agreement. There is nothing corresponding to this in physics. Of course we *can* give *causes* for our laughter, but whether those are in fact the causes is now shown by the person's agreeing that they are. A cause is found experimentally. The psychoanalytic way of finding why a person laughs is analogous to an aesthetic investigation. For the correctness of an aesthetic analysis must be agreement of the person to whom the analysis is given. The difference between a reason and a cause is brought out as follows: the investigation of a reason entails as an essential part one's agreement with it, whereas the investigation of a cause is carried out experimentally. ["What the patient agrees to can't be a *hypothesis* as to the *cause* of his laughter, but only that so-and-so was the *reason* why he laughed."] Of course the person who agrees to the reason was not conscious at the time of its being his reason.
>
> But it is a way of speaking to say the reason was subconscious. It may be expedient to speak in this way, but the subconscious is a hypothetical entity

which gets its meaning from the verifications these propositions have. What Freud says about the subconscious sounds like science, but in fact it is just a *means of representation*. New regions of the soul have not been discovered, as his writings suggest. The display of elements of a dream, for example, a hat (which may mean practically anything) is a display of similes. As in aesthetics, things are placed side by side so as to exhibit certain features. These throw light on our way of looking at a dream; they are reasons for the dream. [But his method of analyzing dreams is not analogous to a method for finding the causes of stomach-ache.] It is a confusion to say that a reason is a cause seen from the inside. A cause is not seen from within or from without. It is found by experiment. [In enabling one to discover the reasons for laughter psychoanalysis provides] merely a representation of processes.[6]

This text condenses all of Wittgenstein's major objections to Freud's enterprise, or perhaps more specifically to the way Freud himself understands, describes, and justifies that enterprise. I shall return later in more detail to the confusion between reasons and causes, which is in a way, from Wittgenstein's perspective, the philosophical confusion par excellence. For the moment what interests me is his way of suggesting that the hypothesis of the unconscious is merely a manner of speaking, which could in principle be discarded without any challenge to what Freud is *really* saying. We might think that Wittgenstein's criticism is unduly radicalized by the way he flirts at this period with the "principle of verification" (the idea that the meaning of a proposition is its method of verification). But the "Conversations on Freud" only repeats exactly the same thing, namely that psychoanalysis, while presenting itself as an experimental discipline, does not satisfy any of the conditions necessary to a discipline of this kind, for reasons that are not accidental but intrinsic. Propositions involving the unconscious are meaningful only insofar as the criteria of (experimental) verification have been adopted for them; and, according to Wittgenstein, this was not done.

Wittgenstein says that using unconscious reasons to explain someone's conduct introduces no radical theoretical innovation in relation to things that we do quite readily anyway, and in no way corresponds to the discovery of still unmapped regions of the soul (the "submerged part" of the mental iceberg). It is entirely possible and legitimate to say that Freud managed to explain certain aspects of our behavior by citing unconscious reasons if we mean by this simply reasons that (1) were not conscious at the moment considered, and (2) can be recognized nonetheless by the person concerned as having been his reasons at the end of a process such as Freud describes. To say that the reasons in question were unconscious and operated unconsciously resembles a hypothesis, but this is in reality only a convenient but false way of describing the end result. The possibility of experimental verification would make the "hypothesis" something more than a simple presentation of the facts; but, precisely, this possibility does not exist, despite the impression Freud gives of having tried and succeeded in experimentally establishing the existence of what he calls the "unconscious."

Wittgenstein makes this point in *The Blue Book* when he compares discussions of the reality of the unconscious with exchanges that take place between realists, idealists, and solipsists, and in a general way between people who disagree on whether to adopt a new system of notation which some propose and others reject, while believing they disagree on the essential facts:

> I shall try to elucidate the problem discussed by realists, idealists and solipsists by showing you a problem closely related to it. It is this: "Can we have unconscious thoughts, unconscious feelings, etc.?" The idea of there being unconscious thoughts has revolted many people. Others again have said that these were wrong in supposing that there could only be conscious thoughts, and that psychoanalysis had discovered unconscious ones. The objectors to unconscious thought did not see that they were not objecting to the newly discovered psychological reactions, but to the way in which they were described. The psychoanalysts on the other hand were misled by their own way of expression into thinking that they had done more than discover new psychological reactions; that they had, in a sense, discovered conscious thoughts which were unconscious. The first could have stated their objection by saying "We don't wish to use the phrase 'unconscious thoughts'; we wish to preserve the word 'thought' for what you call 'conscious thoughts'." They state their case wrongly when they say: "There can only be conscious thoughts and no unconscious ones." For if they don't wish to talk of "unconscious thought," they should not use the expression "conscious thought," either.[7]

Those who identify thought with conscious thought, like the traditional philosophers Freud despairs of convincing, use the word "conscious" without antithesis, that is, in a metaphysical way. And those who claim to have discovered that there really *are* unconscious thoughts, like the psychoanalysts, are in Wittgenstein's view confusing a convention of language, which one can accept or reject, with a revolutionary factual truth that cannot be gainsaid.

Since, as Wittgenstein says, a word has the meaning we give it, it would be patently absurd to claim that the phrase "unconscious thought" can have no meaning. The truth is, it is not because we understand the word "thought" and the word "unconscious" that we automatically understand the phrase "unconscious thought" (that is, make use of it). It has no instant meaning, but neither does it represent an instant contradiction, as certain adversaries of Freud have maintained. The question is only whether a meaning *has* or has not been given; and Wittgenstein has no doubts that the answer is in the affirmative. In another passage of *The Blue Book* he writes:

> It might be found practical to call a certain state of decay in a tooth, not accompanied by what we commonly call toothache, "unconscious toothache" and to use in such a case the expression we have a toothache, but don't know it. It is just in this sense that psychoanalysis talks of unconscious thoughts, acts of volition, etc. Now is it wrong in this sense to say that I have a toothache but don't know it? There is nothing wrong about it, as it is just a new terminology and can at any time be retranslated into ordinary language. On the other hand, this statement clearly uses the word "to know" in a new way" (ibid., pp. 22–23).

The introduction of an expression like "unconscious toothache" by the convention indicated, then, would not be a mistake but might have the inconvenience, among others, of eliciting two sorts of inappropriate reactions. The first would consist of imagining that a "stupendous discovery" has been made, the second of wondering how unconscious pain can indeed be possible. "You may then be tempted to deny the possibility of an unconscious toothache; but the scientist will tell you that it is a proved fact that there is such a thing, and he will say it like a man who is destroying a common prejudice. He will say: 'Surely it's quite simple; there are other things which you don't know of, and there can also be a toothache which you don't know of. It is just a new discovery.' You won't be satisfied, but you won't know what to answer. This situation constantly arises between the scientist and the philosopher" (ibid.).

Freud imagines he is like the scientist here, who has demonstrated—as scientists often do—that something you believed impossible was not only possible but real; but according to Wittgenstein he is really like the philosopher, who, when not protesting that something is impossible, generally rushes to proclaim that an extraordinary discovery has been made. The truth is that, whatever Wittgenstein may think, unconscious thought and unconscious pain may not really be comparable. If by "pain" we mean a person's *mental* state, we will certainly refuse to call (unconscious) pain something that under the circumstances is rather more like a state of the tooth itself. The problem is indeed that these unconscious things must be of a *mental* nature even if they are unconscious. The detractors of the unconscious are often people who think that there is nothing one can call "mental" between the conscious and what is purely neurophysiological or organic (and therefore unconscious simply in the sense that one is not conscious of the existence of dental decay that is not translated into pain). But Wittgenstein means that we might find reasons to say in some cases that we *have* pain although we are not conscious of it. After all, shall we say that anesthesia suppresses the pain itself or that the pain is there but we are simply unable to perceive it? In any case, it is quite possible to credit the idea that we have thoughts that are not conscious, and it is even difficult to avoid it. As Leibniz says: "For ideas are in God from all eternity, and they are in us, too, before we actually think of them. . . . If anyone wants to take ideas to be men's actual thoughts, he may; but he will be gratuitously going against accepted ways of speaking."[8] For Leibniz, what we call "having an idea" is basically in the nature of a faculty or disposition and not a conscious mental state: "The idea . . . consists for us *not in a certain act of thought, but in a faculty*, and we are said to have the idea of a thing even if we are not thinking it, provided we can think of it if the occasion presents itself."[9] Freud says that: "Questioning the existence of the unconscious would be completely unthinkable if one took into consideration all our latent memories" ("The Unconscious," *CP* 4:100). But we are tempted to respond that indeed the word "unconscious" has always been used in this sense. As Leibniz says: "It is . . . one thing to retain, it is another to remember, for the things we retain are not always the things we remember, unless we are reminded of them in some way."[10]

As we have just seen, Wittgenstein supports the idea that Freud really discovered something in the area of psychology, namely "psychological reactions" of a hitherto unknown kind, and as for the rest he simply invented and sought to impose a system of notation that would allow him to redescribe all of psychic life in terms of these new elements. The language of the unconscious, however, says nothing about the facts involved, which may in principle be retranscribed in traditional notation. What psychoanalysis discovered is certainly not the fact that reasons can be hidden from the person who has them, since we commonly explain someone's actions with reasons of this kind. By refining a technique that allows us to induce the subjects to recognize as *theirs* various motives that were hitherto unacknowledged and which they would never have accepted at the outset, we are simply provided with new criteria or new reasons which allow us to say that someone's behavior was determined in a way that the subject was unaware of, by motives that were not conscious. As David Archard notes, a declaration such as, "I see now that all along I unconsciously hated my father, and that it was this unconscious hatred which explained my obsessional need to steal repeatedly," can mean two quite different things:

> The sense of "I see now" can be given as either: "I see now that the only possible explanation for what I have been doing is . . . , though I, of course, do not have now, and have never been aware of, any such feelings"; or: "I see now that I have hated my father, and, while previously I could only steal to express this hatred, I can now face up to these feelings which I have always

had and which I have now become aware of." The first rendering corresponds to a third-person ascription of an unconscious reason; the second to a first-person avowal.[11]

In the first case I admit that the existence of an unconscious reason constitutes the only possible explanation of my behavior, but this is no different from the way I might speak of someone else. In the second I am doing much more than that, since I am describing the result of the process as a conscious grasp of the fact that my behavior was indeed dictated by this reason. Freud acknowledged this distinction by locating the difference between a purely intellectual acceptance of the proposed interpretation (which would not be sufficient to obtain the desired result) and an inner conviction based on the subject's lived experience. But as Archard notes: "Of course the patient's acceptance of the interpretation no more confirms its truth than does that of a disinterested observer acquainted with all the relevant facts. The force of the second 'conviction' depends crucially on what sense, if any, can be given to 'knowing that one has had these feelings all along, albeit unconsciously'" (ibid., p. 127). The problem is not simply to know how an idea that was unconscious can become conscious at a given moment; it is also to understand how the subject can be certain that this idea has simply become conscious and that she has indeed had it all along without being aware of it. This is the problem Wittgenstein raises: in what sense does the patient's recognition that she "now sees" the true reason for her behavior constitute proof that she has discovered, by methods used in such cases, that it was present and operative during the entire period in question?

Hacker contrasts the role played by analogy in fields like aesthetics and art history to its usual role in empirical science. An analogy of the first type consists of comparing architecture with a language and trying to explicate the vocabulary and grammar of this language. Despite its unquestionable richness, such an analogy cannot be regarded as equivalent to, say, the hydrodynamic analogy that has contributed in an important way to progress made in the theory of electricity. An analogy like the linguistic one used in architecture

> does not generate hypotheses that can be tested in experiments, nor does it produce a theory that can be used to predict events. The understanding that is the product of such an analogy is not the result of new information, nor does it lead to new empirical discoveries. It does not lead to the asking of fresh factual questions which can then be answered by further empirical research. It is a new form of description which involves a rearrangement of familiar facts. It makes formal connections between descriptions of architectural features and characterizations of linguistic ones. Thenceforth we can significantly say of architectural features: "That makes sense (or, is nonsensical),"

"This is rhetorical (or, bombastic)," "That is witty (or, ambiguous)," "This is a solecism," and so on. The analogy yields new forms of comparison, changing our understanding of buildings and affecting the way we look at things. We see them under the aspect of the analogical concept. This is a salient feature of aesthetic criticism and description.[12]

According to Wittgenstein, what Freud does is essentially to offer us "good analogies." But these newly minted analogies are typically the sort used by art historians and art critics, not the sort used by physicists. In the language of Hacker (ibid., p. 487), we can say that they are not "model-generating," like the second, but simply "aspect-seeing," like the first. At any rate, this is how Wittgenstein regards them.

According to an interpretation defended by certain Anglo-American philosophers and sometimes regarded as authorized by Wittgenstein's ideas, psychoanalytic explanations are not fundamentally different from our explanations of the human attitudes and behavior, normal or bizarre, which we observe in everyday life. The chief difference consists in the fact that the desires, intentions, motives, etc. invoked by the psychoanalyst are unconscious and can be made conscious only under predetermined conditions, which implies something quite different and much more than a simple effort of attention or reflection on the part of the person concerned. But this difference is not as great as it might initially seem if we agree that it is the nature of unconscious reasons to be available to recognition as such, and that for these too, as Wittgenstein would say, it is essentially the fact of being recognized as such that makes them reasons. If this is the case, there is no need to postulate the existence of a place called "the unconscious" where reasons of this kind are hidden (along with various other elements) while waiting to be summoned undisguised to the consciousness of the subject. As a result, the only use of the vocabulary of the unconscious that is really essential is the adjectival or adverbial use, which is already broadly recognized by ordinary language:

> Where the Freudians are mistaken, according to such a conception, is when they speak of an "unconscious mind" to which elements like those in question belong, and when they employ a causal language to explain their relation to current behavior. They obviously believe that it is necessary to introduce, quite gratuitously, a dubious entity called "the unconscious," when all that is required is the adjectival and adverbial use of "unconscious" to qualify the mental element used in explanations of behavior in the common meaning of the term. The coherent use of the adjective "unconscious" does not necessitate the introduction of the noun, which in itself raises serious and perhaps insoluble philosophical problems (Archard, *Consciousness and the Unconscious*, pp. 125–26).

As Archard notes, the inconvenience of a conception of this kind is that it seems unable to account for the essential distinction that must be made between that which is simply elided from the field of consciousness and that which is repressed. Certain elements are merely temporarily excluded from consciousness and can be retrieved by fairly simple procedures readily available to the subject himself; others are radically excluded from consciousness but nonetheless exercise a continuing influence on behavior. Doesn't Freud say that his theory is rendered irrefutable by "the fact that in the technique of psychoanalysis a means has been found by which the opposing force can be removed and the [unconscious] ideas in question made conscious" (*The Ego and the Id*, p. 12)? The practitioner will probably say that in the course of the analysis he rather literally experiences the action of a resistance that keeps the ideas in question at a distance from consciousness; and in a way it is the fact that he succeeds in annulling the effects of this force that demonstrates his suppression of the force that caused it. If so, once it is admitted that reflection is not the appropriate tool for achieving the desired result, there is the risk of a certain circularity in specifying the conditions that must be fulfilled before individuals can become conscious of the unconscious (repressed) reasons for their acts: "If individuals were not prevented from doing so by their neuroses, they could admit the unconscious reasons for their behavior. But in this case the behavior is neurotic behavior precisely because the unconscious reasons cannot be admitted" (Archard, *Consciousness and the Unconscious*, p. 126). The cure for neurotic behavior is achieved by producing the conditions that make admission possible; and this allows us to identify the impossibility of that admission as having been the cause of the patient's suffering all along.

It may be true that there is good reason to speak of thoughts, desires, acts of volition, and perhaps even pain one has without knowing it; the problem seems to be the shift from "He wanted unconsciously (that is, unknowingly) to kill his father" to "His unconscious wanted him to kill (or wanted to make him kill) his father." "Imagine," writes Wittgenstein, "a language in which, instead of saying 'I found nobody in the room,' one said 'I found Mr. Nobody in the room.' Imagine the philosophical problems which would arise out of such a convention. Some philosophers brought up in this language would probably feel that they didn't like the similarity of the expressions 'Mr. Nobody' and 'Mr. Smith.'" (*The Blue Book*, p. 69). In the same way, some philosophers brought up in the language of psychoanalytic culture might one day discover that they do not much like the resemblance between "the unconscious" and a substantive of the ordinary kind. Wittgenstein also suggests elsewhere that: "We might imagine a language in which one does not say: 'We do not know who did that,' but Mr. Donotknow did that'—so as not to have to say that one does not know something."[13] The philosophical problems that would result from the adoption of conventions of this kind would be quite comparable to those raised by the decision to use the term "unconscious" in a substantive way, and the use—now current—of the substantive "the unconscious."[14] To say that the unconscious did this or that (for example, that it expressed itself in this or that way) is first of all what allows us to avoid saying that we do not know who (or what) has done this. All action must, in effect, have something more than a cause, it must have an author; and bizarre actions cannot have an ordinary author. In our idea of the unconscious we are verging on the mythological with the notion of a hidden agent which has its own desires, wishes, motives, intentions, purposes, ruses, and strategies, and is capable of achieving its ends with an intelligence, skill, and assurance often quite superior to those of the person himself; and while in principle such an agent is entirely unaware of logic and its rules, it reveals itself nonetheless capable of conducting highly subtle arguments. The principle of mythologization lies in our need to find someone or something responsible for everything that happens; so when an action is performed "unconsciously" and therefore cannot be attributed to the conscious subject, we are tempted to look for another author, which it is difficult not to conceive as a conscious agent perfectly aware of what it's doing, though the person concerned is not. However much the psychoanalysts might be tempted to believe, according to Wittgenstein, that they have discovered conscious thoughts which are unconscious, we can suspect them of believing they have discovered a conscious agent, and indeed it could scarcely be more conscious (the unconscious), which is not exactly conscious.

Wittgenstein remarks, apropos the conflict between different "instances," that in the cheating game played between the unconscious and the censor, it is often difficult to tell who is really being cheated:

> The majority of the dreams Freud considers have to be regarded as camouflaged wish fulfilments; and in this case they simply don't fulfil the wish. *Ex hypothesi* the wish is not allowed to be fulfiled, and something else is hallucinated instead. If the wish is cheated in this way, then the dream can hardly be called a fulfilment of it. Also it becomes impossible to say whether it is the wish or the censor that is cheated. Apparently both are, and the result is that neither is satisfied. So that the dream is not an hallucinated satisfaction of anything." (*Lectures and Conversations*, p. 47)

In his "Revision of Dream Theory" (1933), in order to account for the exception represented by the case of traumatic dreams, Freud suggests saying instead that "the dream is the *attempt* to realize a wish." In certain cases "the dream can realize its intention only in a very imperfect way or must simply give it up."[15] Wittgenstein wonders whether we shouldn't say rather that the dream, in the best case, can only be an *attempt* to realize a wish, and the action of the censor an *attempt* to prevent it.

When Freud says of Dostoevsky that the epileptoid attacks he suffered in his youth are explained by an identification with the father figure, that he wished to kill the father and take his place, a wish for which he punishes himself by dying, in a way, in the form of his own father,[16] it is obviously difficult to say where in all this we can locate the cheater and the cheated. As Frank Cioffi notes, Freud's strategy in a case like this bears a strong resemblance to the construction of impossible objects that we find in Escher, and is in its way just as fascinating.[17] More generally we can ask ourselves to what extent the unconscious actually manages to express itself, if only indirectly and in disguised forms dictated by the censor, and to what extent the censor manages to prevent it. True, this is a typical compromise between entirely incompatible demands. The dream, for example, is described as the result of a kind of transaction concluded by two parties mediated by the censor: one speaks in the name of the wish to continue sleeping, the other in the name of a wish that may not be satisfied directly and explicitly. Or, as Freud also says, it is the result of two antagonistic forces, one that produces the wish expressed by the dream and the other that exercises censorship over the wish expressed. Wittgenstein does not question the possibility of seeing things like this. He simply wonders whether the fact that we so willingly accept this way of describing them is any proof of the reality of the entities and processes it postulates.

In an earlier conversation, he notes, apropos the use that Freud makes of the language of conflictual "psychic instances":

> He speaks of overcoming resistance. An "instance" is deluded by another "instance" [Rhees specifies: in the sense in which we speak of a "court of higher instance" (a "court of appeals") that has authority to overrule the judgment of the lower court]. The analyst is supposed to be stronger, able to combat and overcome the delusion of the instance. But there is no way of showing that the whole result of analysis may not be delusion. It is something which people are inclined to accept and which makes it easier for them to go certain ways: this makes certain ways of behaving and thinking natural for them. They have given up one way of thinking and adopted another. (*Lectures and Conversations*, pp. 44–45)

Perhaps, after all, patients suffer from an illusion similar to the dream when they accept the psychoanalyst's explanation as a triumph over the censorship they initially opposed to some unconfessed wish. While Freud is convinced that through rigorously scientific procedures he has managed to reveal a truth which, like most scientific truths, is not very agreeable and may even be unacceptable to most people, Wittgenstein thinks that the explanations he provides have nothing in their favor except the fact that they correspond to a way of thinking which, when proposed to us, seems extremely natural and easily accepted. But none of this proves that things might not be pictured quite differently: "Can we say that we have stripped bare the essential nature of the mind? 'Formation of concept.' Mightn't the whole thing have been treated differently?" (ibid., p. 45). Freud's mistake is to imagine that he did something more than form concepts (or transform those we already had) in a way quite consonant with some of our most natural inclinations. A discipline like physics, for example, succeeds in constructing theories and articulating laws that are justified, when they really are, by something that is quite different from a simple capacity to satisfy a natural demand of this kind. Psychoanalysis is perhaps not, as Kraus suggests, the mental illness whose cure it purports to be; yet it may well be that in some basic way it satisfies a wish that is not exactly what it thinks, and not simply the wish to know the truth about the nature and functioning of our mind. In other words, Freud may show great imagination in the realization of his project, but such imagination is nowhere in evidence when he repeats that his explanations are uniquely suited to account for the facts. This would be true only if we decided to adopt the way of thinking he suggests as the only possible choice.

Some of the criticisms Wittgenstein levels against the theory of instances are rather close to Sartre's and may give the impression of resting on the same kind of incomprehension. Sartre interprets Freud's construction as if he had merely added to the conscious ego a second, alien ego, which cannot be represented unless it too is endowed with a form of consciousness. As Archard says, "There is no doubt too that Sartre reads Freud as if the latter were describing the human mind in terms of multiple personalities" (*Consciousness and the Unconscious*, p. 131). This is clearly not how Freud sees things. For him, the unconscious is not a kind of double of the conscious mind. The conscious and the unconscious are systems of heterogeneous and conflicting forces which obey completely different principles: "The unconscious is not regarded by Freud as *another*, second consciousness, it is fundamentally *other* than, though determinant of, consciousness. In claiming that there is an unconscious, Freud does not employ evidence for the existence of a separate, reasoning mental agent in each of us. Rather, the existence of real psychically efficacious processes of a radically different nature from those of which we are immediately aware must be inferred from the very evidence of the latter" (ibid., p. 35). This is why finally the important distinction seems to be not the heuristic one Freud established between the *conscious*, the *preconscious*, and the *unconscious*, but rather the distinction between primary process, which characterizes the workings of the unconscious as a whole, and secondary process, which characterizes the workings of the preconscious ego. It is true, nonetheless, that Freud regularly characterizes the intervention of the unconscious as the activity of something it is not supposed to be, namely a distinct mental agent whose behavior on many points resembles that of its conscious opposite number. He describes, for example, the position the psychoanalyst occupies in relation to the patient at the time of the cure in the following way: "The analytical physician and the weakened ego of the patient, basing themselves upon the real external world, are to combine against the enemies, the instinctual demands of the id and the moral demands of the consciousness of the superego" (*An Outline of Psychoanalysis*, p. 63). And it is not at all clear that the anthropomorphic mode of expression he uses (notably but not exclusively in his rather "popular" lectures) to describe the confrontation between the different protagonists of the conflict the psychoanalyst must help to resolve can be understood as a simple metaphor which might, in principle, be dispensed with. It seems to play a much more central role. Freud of course dismisses the possibility of assimilating the hypothesis of the unconscious to the postulation of a second ego or a second consciousness. But it is difficult to understand the explanation he gives of normal or pathological phenomena, such as neuroses, dreams, slips, bungled actions, and jokes, etc.,[18] other than in the language of interpersonal conflictual relations, a language that describes a confrontation resolved by a transaction acceptable to both parties, which are represented by two agents in conflict within the person himself. If we accept the Freudian idea that unconscious processes occupy a position in relation to consciousness comparable to those of physical objects that have an objective existence but are not perceived, aren't we admitting to a typical example of animistic projection of the worst kind onto a reality that is in principle "external"? Or at the very least that there is a contradiction between what these objects are supposed to be (the equivalent of unperceived material objects) and what they are? Freud's procedure is questionable, from Wittgenstein's point of view, not, as is sometimes believed, because he reifies but because he personifies the unconscious and, in a more general way, the subpersonal components of the personality.

In *The Psychopathology of Everyday Life*, for example, Freud claims that it is impossible for a number (or a proper name) to be chosen at random. He recounts that in writing to a friend to tell him he had finished correcting the proofs of *The Interpretation of Dreams*, he tells him that he was determined not to change anything else in the text, "even if it contains 2467 mistakes," and then proposes to demonstrate the fact that despite appearances to the contrary, there was nothing arbitrary in the choice of this particular number: "You will find that in the letter I put down the number 2467, as a bold arbitrary estimate of mistakes which will be found in the dream book. . . . However, nothing in the mind is arbitrary or undetermined. You will therefore rightly expect that the unconscious had hastened to determine the number which was left open by consciousness" (*The Psychopathology of Everyday Life*, p. 242). The suggestion here is that even if the conscious mind has not chosen, the unconscious is responsible for doing it (unconsciously) for reasons of its own. The choice did not have conscious reasons, although it could have been entirely determined by causes unknown to the subject, but it had unconscious reasons (and not simply causes). Freud concludes the explanation he found for this case by asserting: "So one can say with justice that not even the number 2467 which I threw out unthinkingly was without its determinants from the unconscious" (ibid., p. 261).

Commentators and critics of Freud have long noted that one of the basic reasons for his difficulty in constructing a stable and satisfying representation of the nature of the mind is the frequent oscillation and constant tension between two analogies or paradigms, one of which, the mechanical, seems to him to correspond to what must be an impersonal, scientific approach to the phenomena in question, while the other, the anthropomorphic, regularly leads him into the realm of what Wittgenstein calls mythology. At certain moments the working of the unconscious is described as obeying objective laws of the purely mechanical type; at others the unconscious is invested with psychological properties similar to those of its owner, and credited with an intentional and intelligent behavior that seems appropriate only to a conscious agent. In both cases it plays the role of a "homunculus" to which concepts are applied that in principle have meaning only on the level of the person viewed as a whole. As certain critics have noted, just as it is I and not my hand who signs a check, things like censorship, repression, etc., if they must be attributed to an agent, can only be related to the entire person and should not be regarded as exercised by only part of one's brain or one's mind, whether the ego, the superego, or anything else. In the language of Daniel Dennett, we might say that despite its status as in principle subpersonal, the unconscious is regularly described in terms that are applicable, strictly speaking, only to the personal level.[19] As Archard says: "On the one hand, the unconscious is an intentional psychic agent which nonetheless behaves in a purely mechanical fashion; on the other hand, the unconscious is cognitively primary, alogical, comprised of shifting and heedless desires, but it makes a very sophisticated use of language" (*Consciousness and the Unconscious*, p. 128). The purely mechanical description, given in terms of the flux, distribution, and discharge of psychic energy, seems to cut the unconscious off definitively from the intentional sphere with which it must nonetheless maintain close relations and within which it must play a fundamentally explanatory role. As for the overtly intentional description, it condemns us, it seems, to commit what Anthony Kenny describes, inspired by Wittgenstein's remarks, as the "homunculus fallacy."[20]

As Archard very aptly notes, there is a direct link between the criticism that invokes the incompatibility of causal and intentional explanations, and the criticism that emphasizes the essentially inappropriate character of any reductionistic attempt to explain what is properly psychic or mental on the basis of something neurophysiological:

> The causal account looks plausible as, and insofar as it is, a neurophysiological account; conversely, the intentional language seems appropriate only to an explanation of the irreducibly mental or psychical. What needs immediately to be said is this: first, the purported inadequacy of Freud's neurophysiological theories should not, and cannot reasonably, be taken to demonstrate the failure of any reductionist account as such; second, opting for a dualist reading of Freud presents problems in terms of its dualism and as an interpretation of Freud. (*Consciousness and the Unconscious*, p. 130)

It would, of course, be quite absurd and dishonest to reproach Freud for failing to solve a problem that is inherent in all theories or philosophies of mind, and which none of them, even the latest and most "scientific," has solved in a really satisfying way. The difficulty he encounters is characteristic of all conceptions that propose to account for personal intentionality and intelligence by trying to derive them from a combination and cooperation of constituents and agents that belong to the personal level and are, in principle, nonintelligent and blind (in any case this is how they must necessarily seem at the ultimate stage of analysis, which will have been cleansed of all the "homunculi" of earlier stages). It is sometimes suggested that Lacan resolved the difficulty inherent in Freud by abandoning once and for all the concessions to vulgar materialism, to reductionism and biologism, and the "unfortunate" borrowings from the language of energetics and crude causality so as to concentrate solely on the properly linguistic nature of the unconscious. I believe, on the contrary, that he has done nothing of the kind, for Lacan uses the phrase the "language of the unconscious" to refer to something that either is not yet a language or simply provides us with a somewhat more sophisticated linguistic version of the same basic aporia. Archard's conclusion on this point seems to me entirely justified:

> It may well be unrealistic to view the unconscious as a linguistically sophisticated, polyglot, culturally educated and super-intelligent agent. And to that extent . . . unreasonable and unnecessary to accept that such an unconscious does exist. But it may not be incoherent. What *is* impossible is to require of language that, for instance, words or signifiers are entirely separate from their

meanings or signifieds; that meaning is to be found in the interrelationship
of words *qua* words. If indeed psychoanalysis does require such a psychoanalytic theory of language and meaning, then arguably psychoanalysis is
incoherent at a level other than that of its theory of mind . . . that may well be
the wholly unintended merit of Lacan's approach" (ibid., p. 132).

If the famous "primacy of the signifier over the signified" means that the
unconscious is sensitive only to the purely phonetic and syntactic properties of signifiers as such, and manipulates them in a way that corresponds
to what might be called a purely formal (and mechanical) treatment, the
normal concept of signification is not really applicable on this level. Meaning cannot result simply from the unstable and respective movements of
signifiers considered only as signifiers. To replace "vulgar" energetics with
a linguistic dynamic of metaphor and metonymy, shifts and slippages of
meaning, etc., and physical or psychological causality with a more abstract and ethereal form of "structural causality," brings us no closer to
the level where we can really introduce notions such as intentionality and
signification properly speaking.

   If we consider that it is the essence of a language to be an activity governed by rules, the formal language of the unconscious is not a language,
because the "linguistic laws" it obeys can be only laws of the causal type,
and not rules. What Lacan needs is a system that functions "like a language" by the application of rules; what he proposes is in fact only a causal
mechanism of a particular sort.[21] The concept of rules, for Wittgenstein,
cannot be completely separate from the idea of a user who knows and
applies the rules. And this means that either the unconscious applies no
rules and speaks no language, or the rules in question on this level are
applied by an agent who knows them or is in principle capable of recogniz-
ing them. It may be that G. P. Baker and P. M. S. Hacker somewhat radicalized Wittgenstein's position when they derived from his remarks on
what it means to "follow a rule" a sort of anticipatory refutation of all the
contemporary theories of language constructed on the idea of rules which
the subject applies without knowing them and which can be discovered
only by the scientific procedure involving the formulation of explanatory
hypotheses and theories on linguistic behavior.[22] But it is clear that if we
are sensitive to Wittgenstein's arguments, we ought to conclude that notions such as *signification, usage, rule, correctness* (or *incorrectness*) of an
application, and so on, are not applicable to the type of "linguistic" activity that is operating, according to Lacan, at the level of the unconscious or
in the unconscious. These two thinkers, then, cannot be reconciled by their
common interest in language and the central importance they attribute to
the problematic of language for the understanding of mental (conscious or
unconscious) phenomena. There are, on the contrary, good reasons to

conclude, as Grahame Lock does, that "Wittgenstein is the 'disciple' of Freud who seems to do nothing but raise objections to his master. Lacan is the 'disciple' of Freud who means to impose a return to Freudian orthodoxy. The question however remains open as to which of these two thinkers may be said to be closest to the spirit of Freud's work. What we might say, in any case, is that with respect to the Lacan of the 1970s at least, Wittgenstein (who died in 1951) may be called an *anti-Lacan avant la lettre*" ("Analytic Philosophy," p. 176).

The "Generalizing Impulse," or the
Philosopher in Spite of Himself

Philosophy is not opposed to science, it behaves like a science and
works in part by the same methods; it departs from it, however, by
clinging to the illusion of being able to present a picture of the world
which is without gaps and is coherent, though one which is bound
to collapse with every fresh advance in our knowledge. It goes astray
in its method by overestimating the epistemological value of our
logical operations and by accepting other sources of knowledge,
such as intuition.

—SIGMUND FREUD, *New Introductory Lectures on Psycho-Analysis* (1933)

I<small>N</small> *An Outline of Psychoanalysis*, Freud uses the following comparison to
justify his conviction that the methods of psychoanalysis are ultimately
comparable to those currently employed in the natural sciences, in particular physics:

> We have adopted the hypothesis of a psychical apparatus extended in space,
> appropriately constructed, developed by the exigencies of life, which gives
> rise to the phenomena of consciousness only at one particular point and under
> certain conditions. This hypothesis has put us in a position to establish psy-
> chology upon foundations similar to those of any other science, such as phys-
> ics. In our science the problem is the same as in the others: behind the attri-
> butes (*i.e.*, qualities) of the object under investigation which are directly
> given to our perception, we have to discover something which is more inde-
> pendent of the particular receptive capacities of our sense organs and which
> approximates more closely to what may be supposed to be the real state of
> things. There is no hope of our being able to reach the latter itself, since it is
> clear that everything new that we deduce must nevertheless be translated
> back into the language of our perceptions, from which it is simply impossible
> for us to set ourselves free. But in this lies the nature and limitation of our

science. It is as though, in physics, we said: "If we could see clearly enough,
we should find that what appear to be solid objects are made up of particles
of such and such shape and size, occupying such and such relative positions."
So we endeavor to increase the efficiency of our sense organs as far as possible
by artificial aids; but it is to be expected that such efforts will fail to affect the
ultimate result. Reality will always remain "unknowable." . . . We have discovered technical methods of filling up the gaps in the phenomena of our
consciousness, and we make use of those methods just as a physicist makes
use of experiment. In this manner we deduce a number of processes which are
in themselves "unknowable" and insert them among the processes of which
we are conscious. And if, for instance, we say: "At this point an unconscious
memory intervened," what this means is: "At this point something occurred
of which we are totally unable to form a conception, but which, if it had
entered our consciousness, could only have been described in such and such
a way."[1]

This comparison is questionable for the following reason: even if physics does try to construct a more or less accurate representation of the way
abstract objects mentioned in the theory might appear to us if they became
accessible to perception (this is one of the imperatives which the construction of "models" for the theory must obey), it is certainly not bound to
describe these objects in terms we would use if we perceived them as they
really are. On the contrary, it has ways of characterizing them that are
independent of any reference to the possibility of perception. Besides,
some of these objects are not only in practice but also in principle and by
nature incapable of being the objects of any sort of perception whatever.
They are therefore very different from unconscious processes, whose description remains, Freud tells us, fundamentally dependent on the language used for conscious processes—with which they are thought to be
analogous. Psychoanalytic theorizing, then, is ultimately ungrounded, for
reasons inherent in the irreducible and unexplained fact of consciousness,
in a way that seems to have no equivalent in a science like physics.

Wittgenstein's general lack of enthusiasm for science, and for a culture
dominated like ours by scientific thinking, occasionally suggests that his
concept of what a science is, broadly speaking, might have been much
looser or more accommodating than that of the members of the Vienna
Circle or Karl Popper. His diagnosis of the case of psychoanalysis, however, is clear evidence to the contrary. It is essentially in relation to the
example of physics that Wittgenstein, like Popper, judges the pretensions
of psychoanalysis to the status of experimental science; and his verdict is
no less harsh, even if his arguments are different and his final judgment
more positive. For Wittgenstein, too, it is obvious that, whatever Freud
thought, there is a world of difference between what he is doing and what
is being done by scientists in the disciplines to which he refers. And con-

trary to what some people would like to believe, there is every indication that Wittgenstein was not more tolerant but, on the contrary, more severe than certain members of the Vienna Circle in terms of his attitude toward certain typical forms of pseudo-science. Neider reports that the break with Carnap was the result of Wittgenstein's discovery in Carnap's library of a work by Schrenck-Notzing devoted to the study of certain parapsychological phenomena (cf. "Gesprach mit Heinrich Neider," p. 23). Wittgenstein simply could not understand how anyone could waste his time on such nonsense, even out of simple "scientific" curiosity. His distrust of the natural sciences never meant that he believed in the possibility of another sort of science that might claim to rival official science by using completely different methods of its own; nor did his distrust imply any sympathy for the idea of a philosophic "science" different from the science of scientists and more profound.

I have already mentioned the singular contrast between Breuer's scientific prudence (some would probably say cowardice) and Freud's speculative boldness (or temerity). Contrary to popular wisdom on the subject, this element played a much more defining role in their relations than Breuer's purported repugnance at the idea that sexuality holds a central place in the etiology of hysteria and neuroses in general. Breuer himself emphasizes that *"the great majority of severe neuroses in women have their origin in the marriage bed"* (in *Studies on Hysteria*, p. 246), and that although the nonsexual affects of fright, anxiety, and anger lead to the development of hysterical phenomena, it is nonetheless indispensable to keep in mind that "the sexual factor is by far the most important and the most productive of pathological results" (ibid.). Freud's explanation of the growing disaffection and the final break between the two men is at the very least, then, rather implausible. It must come as something of a surprise, in any case, to see Freud assert thirty years later: "It would have been difficult to guess from the *Studies on Hysteria* what an importance sexuality has in the aetiology of the neuroses."[2] What really happened between Breuer and Freud is surely described much more accurately by saying that "Breuer's collaboration with Freud came to an end when Freud began to insist that sexuality was the essential cause of *every* hysteria as well as of most other neuroses" (Sulloway, *Freud, Biologist of the Mind*, p. 85).

Freud himself explained that he did not really understand why Breuer "had kept his knowledge secret for so long, which seemed to me invaluable, instead of adding to the riches of science" (ibid., p. 52). Freud simply did not understand the scruples that prevented Breuer from generalizing and publishing his results as quickly as possible. "The next question," he writes, "was whether one could generalize what he had discovered on the basis of a single case of illness. The state of things he had brought to light seemed to me so fundamental that I could not believe it would be absent in any case of hysteria, once it had been demonstrated in a single case. But this is something that could only be determined by experiment" (ibid.). One of the most consistent characteristics of Freud's enterprise is his remarkable conviction that it is enough to examine a single well-chosen case, or a very small number of cases, to know instantly what is necessarily fundamental and essential in all other cases. Freud reasons like a man who is convinced that once the right explanation (his own) is accepted, it will be understood that there is basically only one kind of hysteria, dream, parapraxis, joke, and so on. He behaves, in Wittgenstein's view, not like a proper scientist but rather like a philosopher who is convinced that he must and can explain the resemblances that exist between a multitude of cases, which can be very different in other respects, by the recognition (or rather the postulation) of an extremely general quality that is common to all of them but hidden at a certain depth beneath the diversity of appearances.

We should not be surprised, then, to see Wittgenstein regularly compare the universal propositions of Freudian theory, not to ordinary scientific hypotheses, which would require testing and confirmation, but rather to generalizations of the sort that generate the most typical philosophic theories:

> Now when, as in the case of Freud, a generalization is seized upon . . . dreams are not simply wish-fulfilment, they are *fundamentally* or *in essence* . . . wish-fulfilment. Classifications are introduced. There may be clear wish-fulfilment, not so clear, dark wish-fulfilment, etc. And so with hedonism. Pleasures are not all of the same kind. There are higher and lower. . . . We desire nothing but pleasure, but there are qualities of pleasure. (Bouwsma, *Conversations, 1949–1951*, pp. 59–60)

Freud simply does not manage to take seriously the possibility that he might have found a satisfying explanation for a certain kind of dream, but not for all dreams:

> Freud was influenced by the 19th century idea of dynamics—an idea which has influenced the whole treatment of psychology. He wanted to find some one explanation which would show what dreaming is. He wanted to find the *essence* of dreaming. And he would have rejected any suggestion that he might be partly right but not altogether so. If he was partly wrong, that would have meant for him that he was wrong altogether—that he had not really found the essence of dreaming" (Wittgenstein, *Lectures and Conversations*, p. 48).

Wittgenstein sees no contradiction between the physical or physiological explanation of dreaming and Freud's kind of explanation, or between

methods of treating mental illness that correspond to those two entirely
different approaches to the same phenomena; he simply maintains that if
we put ourselves in Freud's place, we can imagine explanations quite different from his. This is what he explains to Drury in a conversation in
1948:

> I have been thinking about the physical methods of treatment that you em-
> ploy. There is no contradiction between this approach and that of Freud. If I
> have a dream, it may be due to some physical cause, something I have eaten
> for supper that has disagreed with me. But what I dream about, the contents
> of the dream, may have a psychological explanation. It seems to me that my
> dreams are always an expression of my fears, not, as Freud thought, my
> wishes. I could build up an interpretation of dreams just as cogent as Freud's
> in terms of repressed fears." (Drury, "Conversations with Wittgenstein,"
> p. 168)

The kind of determined response one hopes to elicit when trying to identify
the cause of a phenomenon has no validity when explaining its contents.

In his *Remarks on Colour*, Wittgenstein cites the Freudian idea of
dreaming as disguised wish fulfillment as an example of "primary phenomena" interpreted in a dogmatic and partial way: "The primary
phenomenon ('*Urphänomen*') is, e.g., what Freud thought he recognized
in simple wish-fulfilment dreams. The primary phenomenon is a precon-
ceived idea that takes possession of us."[3] Freud proceeded on this point
just as Goethe thought he could in dealing with the phenomenon of color.
Having discovered particularly clear examples of dreams that could be
regarded as constituting the camouflaged fulfillment of a wish, Freud postulated that the same basic phenomenon should be found in all examples
of dreams. We might say, in the language of Goethe, that what he held
against Breuer was the latter's incapacity to bow before the evidence of the
first phenomenon and immediately draw from a single, exemplary case, or
very few cases, conclusions valid in all cases.

In order to understand what Wittgenstein means, it may be useful to
cite one of the most significant remarks Goethe makes about the *Urphänomen*:

> "The Urphänomen:
> ideal as the ultimate knowledge,
> real as known,
> symbolic because it includes all cases,
> identical with all cases."   (*Maximen und Reflexionen*, sec. 869)

Wittgenstein regards the *Urphänomen* as essentially symbolic in the
sense that it corresponds to the adoption of a model or prototype to be
used in the description of phenomena (*all* phenomena), and for this very

THE "GENERALIZING IMPULSE"

reason it can be neither ideal nor real nor identical (to all the cases it allows us to identify) in the sense that Goethe intends. Wittgenstein's objection to the way Freud treats the phenomenon of the dream is finally the same sort of objection he makes to the morphology of Spengler's universal history: "the prototype [*Urbild*] ought to be clearly presented for what it is; so that it characterizes the whole discussion and determines its form. This makes it the focal point, so that its general validity will depend on the fact that it determines the form of discussion rather than on the claim that everything which is true only of it holds too for all the things that are being discussed" (*Culture and Value*, p. 14). In Freud, the model of the dream-as-disguised-wish-fulfillment is not presented for what it is, namely a principle that determines the form of discussion of all the phenomena concerned, but as corresponding to the discovery of the real nature of dreaming; and it is applied to all dreams, not because it has been demonstrated by a scientific investigation of different kinds of dreams, but because it has been granted a privileged place in the discussion.

What happens, then, is not that Freud's hypotheses are confirmed by evidence that might in principle just as easily contradict them, but rather that the grammar of any likely explanation or reason has been fixed so that a completely different kind of explanation or reason cannot be accepted for consideration as *the* explanation or *the* reason. Freud does not hesitate to state that in certain cases an apparent counterexample has been produced simply by the (unconscious) wish to refute the theory he is advancing; and this is immediately transformed into a supplementary confirmation. He writes: " 'Counter-wish dreams' that are apparently in direct contradiction to the theory of the dream as the disguised fulfilment of a wish appear regularly in the course of my treatments when a patient is in a state of resistance to me; and I can count almost certainly on provoking one of them after I have explained to a patient for the first time my theory that dreams are fulfilments of wishes" (*The Interpretation of Dreams*, SE 4:157–58). Furthermore, it is curious to note that Freud is clearly much less eager to admit the possibility of dreams of compliance, which might be provoked by the patient's wish to offer additional confirmation of the theory he articulates. Yet, as Cioffi remarks: "If a patient was capable of producing a dream in order that it might appear to contradict Freud's theories, why should not another patient produce one in order to confirm them?"[4] At another moment, however, after having dismissed several pages earlier the objection of the skeptic who fears that the dreamer has dreams of a certain kind only because he knows he should have them, Freud readily admits that

in many dreams which recall what has been forgotten and repressed, it is impossible to discover any other unconscious wish [that of pleasing the analyst] to which the motive force for the formation of the dream can be attributed. So that if anyone wishes to maintain that most of the dreams that can be made use of in analysis are compliant dreams and owe their origin to suggestion, nothing can be said against that opinion from the point of view of analytical theory."[5]

In the absence, then, of any other unconscious wish that might explain the formation of the dream, one could always invoke the wish simply to oblige the psychoanalyst, thereby providing cheap confirmation of the theory once again. Freud immediately adds, however, that the explanations given in the *Introductory Lectures on Psychoanalysis* (Lecture 28) on the relation of the transference to suggestion ought to demonstrate "to what degree the acknowledgement of the effect of suggestion in our sense is hardly likely to compromise the reliability of our results" (*SE* 16:267). The basic argument countering the objection based on the psychoanalyst's power of suggestion is, broadly, that the analyst can influence the particular mode of expression the patient's unconscious might use, but certainly not what it expresses—his unconscious itself. Freud readily admits that the manifest content of dreams is, as one would expect, influenced by the analytic cure, and that their latent content can be as well, but only to the extent that "one part of those latent thoughts of the dream corresponds to formations of preconscious thoughts, perfectly capable of becoming conscious, by which the dreamer would have been able eventually to react, even during the evening, to the incitements of the analyst, that the responses of the analysand go in the same direction as these or against them" (*SE* 16:264). In other words, "one never manages to exercise any influence over the mechanism of dream formation itself, or over the dreamwork properly speaking; this is a point we can regard as firmly established" (ibid.). But unfortunately, the passage cited above concerning dreams of compliance seems difficult to reconcile with this reassuring conviction that the psychoanalyst never acquires any real power over the mechanism of dream formation itself.

Sebastiano Timpanaro cites the lecture on "The Dream-work" (Lecture II of the *Introductory Lectures*) as an example to support the following judgment: "The actual non-scientificity of the theory resides precisely in its capacity to elude (by way of sophistry) every possibility of falsification. Perhaps most capricious and scientifically dishonest of all is Freud's 'proof' that all dreams, even anxiety dreams, are expression of a repressed wish."[6] Timpanaro points out that the weakness of Freud's theory of dreams is not that it is frequently contradicted by facts it fails to take into account, which would make it a scientific theory comparable to others and just as respectable, but that, on the contrary, it has a way of escaping any possibility of falsification:

Does someone have an anxiety dream about the death of a beloved person? Have no fear; this too is a wish-fulfillment, for it represents a resurgence of archaic psychic material which reveals that at some point in the infantile life of the dreamer the death of that person was indeed desired. The anxiety dream is concerned with the dreamer's *own* death? Another case of a wish— this time for self-punishment because of a guilt complex." (Timpanaro, *The Freudian Slip*, p. 218)

We might say the problem is not to demonstrate convincingly that this or that dream is indeed the fulfillment of a wish, but rather given any dream, to find a wish it might be thought to fulfill. And there are such different and contradictory wishes the subject might seek unconsciously to satisfy (including, if need be, that of placating or contradicting the psychoanalyst) that the difficulty ought not to be insurmountable. Thus, for example, "even punishment-dreams are wish-fulfilments, but they do not fulfil the wishes of the instinctual impulses, but those of the critical, censuring and punishing functions of the mind" (*New Introductory Lectures*, p. 43). Freud confidently concludes that to his knowledge, "dreams that take place in traumatic neurosis are the only real exception and dreams of punishment the single apparent exception to the tendency of the dream to fulfill a wish" ("Remarks upon the Theory and Practice of Dream Interpretation," p. 267). If anything is more astounding than the acknowledgment of a single real exception, it is surely the certainty of encountering only a single *apparent* exception when these seem at first glance so abundant. But instead of accusing Freud, as Timpanaro does, of characteristic dishonesty, it would probably be more helpful to follow Wittgenstein and speak of the way the grammar of the description has been permanently fixed, leaving the theorist no other choice and, despite appearances, proscribing any form of fantasy or "caprice." At any rate, it is unlikely that the example cited above, which eliminates a direct counterexample by immediately reinterpreting it as the disguised fulfillment of a wish to refute the psychoanalyst, would convince anyone who had not already granted the universal applicability of Freud's explanation. Even if we find Popper's criticism of Freud a little too simplistic and dogmatic, we must admit that it is quite difficult to imagine a counterexample that is likely to constitute a serious, much less insoluble problem for Freud's dream theory.

A reasonably skeptical reader of *The Interpretation of Dreams* will be quick to wonder whether Freud actually tried to test his theory or ever *really* managed to do so. The kind of cleverness he employs as a last resort to dispose of certain inconvenient facts amply demonstrates that what he did was rather, in the language of Wittgenstein, to propose a "concept formation" (*Begriffsbildung*) and adopt a method of description that is universally applicable, not because over time the facts have been shown to

conform to the theory, but rather because of the initial decision to concep-
tualize them and describe them in this way. The counterexamples treated
are in reality much less a threat to the contents of the theory itself than a
challenge to interpretive ingenuity, and successfully raised each time by
the theorist. Freud simply urges us to accept a conceptual connection we
hadn't yet suspected between the dream and the fulfillment of a wish. He
tries to persuade us to regard dreaming henceforth in this way; but he does
not demonstrate, and really has no need to demonstrate, that every dream
is indeed a wish fulfillment. The adoption of such a system of representation usually amounts to the decision to describe all subsequent cases that
might arise in terms of a predetermined paradigm, meaning in some cases
in terms of greater or lesser significant deviations (which one can hope to
explain in another way) from the paradigm. But in the case of Freud's
essentialist explanation of the nature of dreaming, we quickly realize that
all deviations will be merely apparent. Even anxiety dreams *are* really
wish-fulfillment dreams in the end.

Like most philosophical theories, the Freudian construction rests,
above all, on the characteristic tendency to generalize or universalize the
clear case:

> We now have a *theory*, a "dynamic theory" of the proposition; of language,
> but it does not present itself to us as a theory. For it is the characteristic thing
> about such a theory that it looks at a special clearly intuitive case and says:
> "*That* shows how things are in every case; this case is the exemplar of *all*
> cases."—"Of course! It has to be like that" we say, and are satisfied. We have
> arrived at a form of expression that *strikes us as obvious*. But it is as if we had
> now seen something lying *beneath* the surface.[7]

We understand perfectly why Wittgenstein takes issue with Freud when
we remember what he says about the way he himself believed, writing the
Tractatus, that he had succeeded in elucidating the nature of the proposition by presenting it as a picture of the fact it represents: "The basic evil
of Russell's logic, as also of mine in the *Tractatus*, is that what a proposition is is illustrated by a few commonplace examples, and then pre-
supposed as understood in full generality."[8] The proposition according to
which "*every* dream is the disguised fulfillment of a wish" is, in sum, the
same type as the statement in the *Tractatus*: "*Every* proposition is the
picture of a fact," and equally unsatisfying. "I once said," Wittgenstein
notes, "that a proposition is a picture of reality. This might introduce a
very useful way of looking at it, but it is nothing else than saying, I want
to look at it as a picture" (*Wittgenstein's Lectures, 1932–1935*, p. 108n.).
This is just what Freud does when it comes to dreaming. Unfortunately, in
both cases the adoption of an extremely general mode of description seems
and is wrongly interpreted to correspond to the discovery of a no less gen-

eral fact that provides an underlying unity to the multiplicity of surface phenomena which philosophical understanding is not ready to accept. Under the circumstances, it is not difficult to understand why Wittgenstein found Freud so interesting from the philosophical point of view. In a lecture devoted to Freud's book, *Jokes and Their Relation to the Unconscious*, "He says that Freud's book on this subject was a very good book for looking for philosophical mistakes, and that the same was true of his writings in general, because there are so many cases in which one can ask how far what he says is a 'hypothesis' and how far merely a good way of representing a fact—a question as to which he said Freud is constantly unclear."[9]

Wittgenstein, then, does not believe that psychoanalytic explanations are accepted on the basis of abundant and varied evidence, even if they can give and were intended by Freud to give that impression:

> Take Freud's view that anxiety is always a repetition in some form of the anxiety we felt at birth. He does not establish this by reference to evidence— for he could not do so. But it is an idea which has a marked attraction. It has the attraction which mythological explanations have, explanations which say that this is all a repetition of something that happened before. And when people do accept or adopt this, then certain things seem much clearer and easier for them. (*Lectures and Conversations*, p. 43)

Wittgenstein styles himself a "follower" of Freud, as it were; but he does not, as we have seen, believe that the existence of the unconscious itself was proven or even made sufficiently probable by the kind of facts and arguments Freud was convinced he had abundantly supplied: "So it is with the notion of the unconscious also. Freud does claim to find evidence in memories brought to light in analysis. But at a certain stage it is not clear how far such memories are due to the analyst. In any case, do they show that the anxiety was necessarily a repetition of the original anxiety?" (ibid.).

Wittgenstein's criticism is surely very different from Popper's, and more astute; but it is no less radical or less sensitive to the argument of the "Oedipal complex," and to the idea that a good number of empirical confirmations invoked to support psychoanalytic hypotheses may result simply from the psychoanalyst's powers of suggestion over the patient, and thus be contaminated much more than they would be by the theory itself. What makes Freud's explanations immediately convincing and even rather irresistible in the eyes of many people corresponds rather, according to Wittgenstein, to something that preexists any idea of verification or refutation properly speaking, and remains, despite appearances, fundamentally independent of such an idea.

At a certain moment in his correspondence with Einstein, Freud poses the following questions: "It may seem to you as though our theories are a kind of mythology and, in the present case, not even an agreeable one. But does not every science come in the end to a kind of mythology like this? Cannot the same be said to-day of your own physics?"[10] Freud has just explained that "with a little license to speculate" we can postulate the existence of a death wish in the human heart that leads to an inanimate state and is the source of the aggressive and destructive tendencies of human beings. He himself compares this rather dubious sort of explanation to a form of mythology. What is curious is his way of assuming that physics—probably at its most "speculative"—might find itself in the same sort of situation. If science as a whole could be branded as merely a kind of mythology, it would be hard to understand Freud's stubborn attempt to gain recognition for psychoanalysis as a scientific theory. It is certainly no easier to distinguish between a scientific mythology and a mythology that is not scientific than between a science and a pseudo-science. One of the most disconcerting arguments used regularly against people who contest the scientific character of psychoanalysis has consisted of remarking that science itself, all things considered, is no more "scientific." Clearly translated, this argument is an attempt to preserve a cherished distinction (between a scientific enterprise like psychoanalysis and an approach that takes its bearings from speculation or myth pure and simple) by invoking as a final strategy the notion that this distinction is completely vague or simply doesn't exist.

Freud concedes that: "The theory of instincts is, so to say, our mythology. Instincts are mythical entities magnificent in their indefiniteness" (*New Introductory Lectures*, p. 95). When Wittgenstein qualifies psychoanalysis itself as a "powerful mythology" (*Lectures and Conversations*, p. 52), he evidently doesn't mean to pronounce the kind of radical condemnation that such a designation might suggest; but nonetheless his attitude, as a result, is antithetical to one that would compare the situation of psychoanalysis with that of the sciences. Mythology is, of course, not altogether absent from the sciences, since the mythological character of an explanation depends much less on its crude, naive, or overly speculative character than on its capacity to impress people as being the universally valid explanation, convincing a priori because of the desire, and not the thought, that it should be able to account for every case. The distinguishing feature of psychoanalysis, in Wittgenstein's view, is that it never really manages to go beyond this initial stage. Despite its claims, it never arrives at the formulation of causal laws that might be confronted with proper experimental evidence. The framework it sets up is not appropriate to, and does not lead to the formulation of, scientific laws, although it is understood that there must be laws of this kind in the realm of mental life, just as in the world of physics. Wittgenstein does not take the trouble to discuss this point at length, since it seems obvious to him.

In "Wittgenstein's Lectures in 1930–33" (in Moore), he maintains that: "Freud did not in fact give any method of analysing dreams which was analogous to the rules which will tell you what are the causes of stomach ache" (p. 316). But in one of the "Conversations on Freud," in which he contrasts what psychoanalytic explanations really do with what they give the impression of doing, he evokes the possibility of a treatment of the dream that might be qualified as scientific: "On the other hand, one might form an hypothesis. On reading a report of the dream, one might predict that the dreamer can be brought to recall such and such memories. And this hypothesis might or might not be verified. This might be called a scientific treatment of the dream" (*Lectures and Conversations*, p. 46). It is regrettable that Wittgenstein does not linger a little longer over this crucial point, since apparently numerous examples can be cited in which Freud gives the impression of indeed formulating hypotheses of the kind Wittgenstein evokes and then actually trying to verify them. Both because of the impossibility of proving that the verifying evidence is really independent and not simply the product of suggestion, and because of the essential and unusual role in authenticating the experimenter's conclusions played by the "object" of study, Wittgenstein is obviously not prepared to concede that anyone can really speak of "verifications."

It is true that, as Cioffi remarks, it is difficult to be entirely reassured on this point if we look closely at the kind of validation Freud invokes to bolster certain of his most famous "historical" reconstructions:

> We find that either the events or scenes reconstructed have too great an independent probability to support the validity of the interpretive technique (as with Dora's urinary incontinence), or were known independently of the analysis (as with the severe beating Paul had from his father and the castration threats to which little Hans was exposed). The apparent exception to this is, what is often regarded as Freud's greatest reconstructive achievement, his discovery that a patient, at the age of 18 months, saw his parents engage in "a coitus a tergo, thrice repeated,"[11] at five in the afternoon. This certainly doesn't lack circumstantiality, what it lacks is corroboration. Freud is aware of this and falls back on a coherence argument." ("Wittgenstein's Freud," pp. 201–202)

Wittgenstein himself thinks that the psychoanalyst is primarily in search of a "good" story that will produce the desired therapeutic effect once it is accepted by the patient, and yet neither the patient's assent nor therapeutic success in itself proves that this story is true or even should be true.

According to Moore's report, in Wittgenstein's discussion of the Freudian explanation of the joke he explained that the patient who agrees to the psychoanalyst's explanation as to why he laughed "did not think of this reason at the moment when he laughed, and that to say that he thought of it 'subconsciously' tells you nothing as to what was happening at the moment when he laughed" ("Wittgenstein's Lectures in 1930–33," p. 317). The proposed psychogenic explanation of the joke's effect on the listener therefore tells us nothing, properly speaking, about what may have happened in his mind at the moment in question, though this is precisely what it is supposed to tell us. In the event, then, what point is there in speaking of unconscious processes that take place at a given moment in the mind? In his *Lectures, Cambridge 1932–1935*, Wittgenstein compares the role played by unconscious mental events in Freud's system to that played by invisible masses in the system of Hertz. In both cases we are dealing with what he calls a "norm of expression," which guarantees the possibility of a very general description:

> Whenever we say that something *must* be the case we are using a norm of expression. Hertz said that wherever something did not obey his laws there must be invisible masses to account for it. This statement is not right or wrong, but may be practical or impractical. Hypotheses such as "invisible masses," "unconscious mental events," are norms of expression. They enter into language to enable us to say there *must* be causes. (They are like the hypothesis that the cause is proportional to the effect. If an explosion occurs when a ball is dropped, we say that some phenomenon must have occurred to make the cause proportional to the effect. On hunting for the phenomenon and not finding it, we say that it has merely not yet been found.) We believe we are dealing with a natural law *a priori*, whereas we are dealing with a norm of expression that we ourselves have fixed. (p. 16).

We might reproach Freud, then, not for having placed a universal norm of expression at the head of his system, since that is usual scientific procedure, but rather for having done nothing more than that. Furthermore, its justification on pragmatic grounds is, finally, much less important than our irresistible propensity to accept it. Psychoanalysis offers us nothing more, in Wittgenstein's view, than a system of representation or a method of description for the facts in a particular category, while a discipline like physics, even if it also begins this way, does not stop there but pushes through to the formulation of empirical hypotheses that can really be tested. This being so, Wittgenstein's general treatment of the sciences tends to undermine rather than enhance the strict distinction he is trying to establish between the situation of psychoanalysis and that of a discipline like physics. In his *Lectures, Cambridge 1932–1935*, he describes the revolutionary change introduced by Copernicus in the following way:

> Something may play a predominant role in our language and be suddenly removed by science, e.g., the word "earth" lost its importance in the new Copernican notation. Where the old notation had given the earth a unique position, the new notation put lots of planets on the same level. Any obsession arising from the unique position of something in our language ceases as soon

as another language appears which puts that thing on a level with other things. (p. 98)

And he specifies in a footnote:

It might be said that Copernicus discovered certain facts about the planets, and that it was the discovery of these facts which removed the obsession about the earth and not the change from Ptolemy's notation. But the new facts might still have been expressed, in a complicated way, in Ptolemy's notation and the obsession not removed. On the other hand, the obsession might have been removed had Copernicus made up a notation with the sun as center, even though it had no application. Of course Copernicus did not *think* about notations but about planets. (Ibid.)

Although Wittgenstein did not doubt that Copernican theory was concerned with real objects (the planets) and not with elements of notation, he is not always very clear about what distinguishes a theory like Copernicus's from a simple system of notation. "What a Copernicus or a Darwin really achieved was not the discovery of a true theory but of a fertile new point of view" (*Culture and Value*, p. 18). But this, of course, is also Freud's real merit; and if we focus only on this, the difference between his case and that of Copernicus or Darwin (to whom Wittgenstein compares him) is far from obvious. Like Copernicus and Darwin, Freud offers us a different system of notation in which an element that had occupied a central position (the conscious ego) is dispossessed of this privileged place. But what, we might ask, have Copernicus and Darwin done, exactly, to justify our conviction that they have made an essential contribution to science, whereas Freud, if we believe Wittgenstein, offers us only a purely speculative construction?

We generally agree that Wittgenstein directly anticipated the Kuhnian theory that the change of the scientific paradigm corresponds to the perception of a new aspect, or a rather unexpected sort of *Gestalt-switch*. When a new paradigm is adopted, it is clearly not because it conforms more closely to the facts, since obviously the question of verification cannot yet be posed, and moreover it probably has meaning only within a determined paradigm. But what justifies the unusual severity with which the change of paradigm introduced by Freud tends to be judged? If we think, as Feyerabend does, that revolutionary scientific theories (for example, Galileo's) are imposed essentially through persuasion and propaganda well before real arguments can be advanced in their favor, and in any case well before they are effectively tested, we are likely to conclude that Freud's case is not on the whole very different from that of Galileo or any other scientific revolutionary. In such instances the faults for which Breuer tended to reproach Freud would even look like eminent and absolutely indispensable scientific virtues, virtues which Breuer himself lamentably lacked. This would surely be our view if we took as our working assumption that Freud really did create a new and revolutionary science. Wittgenstein, as we have seen, thinks this is not the case; and his reticences and philosophical criticisms are on some points rather similar to those Breuer formulated from the "ordinary" scientific point of view.

Wittgenstein does not tell us explicitly whether he considers Darwinian theory itself a scientific one. If science is at issue, evolutionary theory too is a science that does not formulate causal laws; and yet without abusively assimilating explanation to prediction, we might have difficulty saying that it has no real explanatory power. Its chief merit, as Wittgenstein recognizes, and which is also the merit of Freudian theory, is the way it gives us an illuminating synoptic presentation (*eine übersichtliche Darstellung*, as he calls it, the kind of thing philosophy looks for in the field of concepts) of an enormous multiplicity of facts which at first appear to be completely disparate.[12] What is important in both cases is not the "historic" aspect of the proposed explanation, the genetic and causal connections and the relations of provenance and of real derivation, but the conceptual connections and formal transformations: "I can see the evolutionary hypothesis as nothing more, as the clothing of a formal connection."[13] And as in the case of psychoanalysis, Wittgenstein remarks that the reasons why Darwinian theory was accepted (at that time) have little to do with any elements of verification, which are certainly not sufficient to induce such conviction:

32. Cf. the Darwinian upheaval. One circle of admirers who said: "Of course," and another circle [of enemies—R] who said: "Of course not." Why in the Hell should a man say "of course"? (The idea was that of monocellular organisms becoming more and more complicated until they become mammals, men, etc.) Did anyone see this? No. Has anyone seen it happening now? No. The evidence of breeding is just a drop in the bucket. But there were thousands of books in which this was said to be *the* obvious solution. People were *certain* on grounds which were extremely thin. Couldn't there have been an attitude which said: "I don't know. It is an interesting hypothesis which may eventually be well confirmed"? This shows how you can be persuaded of a certain thing. In the end you forget entirely every question of verification, you are just sure it must have been like that.

33. If you are led by psycho-analysis to say that really you thought so and so or that really your motive was so and so, this is not a matter of discovery, but of persuasion. In a different way you could have been persuaded of something different. Of course, if psycho-analysis cures your stammer, it cures it, and that is an achievement. One thinks of certain results of psycho-analysis as a discovery Freud made, as apart from something persuaded to you by a psycho-analyst, and I wish to say this is not the case. (*Lectures and Conversations*, pp. 26–27)

We see that in addition to the crucial analogy that leads him to compare the two cases, there is also a significant difference in the way Wittgenstein treats them. He does not exclude the possibility that the Darwinian hypothesis (which must really be one) may one day achieve the status of a well-confirmed hypothesis. "Verification" may come later and perhaps long afterward (as it has indeed done). But unlike a good number of philosophers and even some students of the "hard" sciences, Wittgenstein does not feel the need to delve into a deeper and more detailed examination of what might be said from a properly epistemological point of view about the case of psychoanalysis (not surprising if we remember that philosophy of science was hardly his central concern). What he does say on this point remains very schematic, and we might even suspect him of sometimes confusing the generic hypotheses of the theory (which we would have to locate at a specific level in the construction of the theory, and if necessary imagine a way to test them) with the particular hypotheses the psychoanalyst is led to formulate and verify in the course of the cure. But he is clearly convinced that because of the very nature of the analyst-patient relationship (and perhaps the reader's with Freud), the "evidence" in the case of psychoanalysis is and always will be essentially the product of successful persuasion.

Clark Glymour remarks on this point: "Whether or not one thinks as I do that on the whole Freud's arguments for psychoanalytic theory are dreadful, it is a mistake to think that the quality and nature of his arguments are uniform, let alone that they are uniformly bad."[14] Glymour maintains that the analysis of the Rat Man case provides an example of the "bootstrap strategy," which entirely merits comparison with procedures used by the most rigorous scientists: "The Rat Man case . . . is largely cogent, free of obvious indoctrination of the patient, and has rather few arbitrary conclusions within it. . . . My claim, unlikely as it may sound, is that the major argument of the Rat Man case is not so very different from the major argument of Book III of Newton's *Principia*" (*Theory and Evidence*, p. 265). In other words, according to Glymour: "The strategy involved in the Rat Man case is essentially the same as a strategy very frequently used to test physical theories. Further, this strategy, while simple enough, is more powerful than the hypothetico-deductive-falsification strategy described for us by so many philosophers of science."[15] But to be thorough we must add that while the Rat Man case gives Freud an occasion to modify his theory in order to account for recalcitrant evidence, the resulting change would be difficult to regard, from the epistemological point of view, as a decided improvement:

In *Totem and Taboo*, four years after the Rat Man case appeared, Freud emphasized that the guilt that obsessional neurotics feel is guilt over a happening that is psychically real but need not actually have occurred. By 1917 Freud not only listed phantasies themselves as etiological factors alternative to real childhood sexual experiences, but omitted even the claim that the former are usually or probably based on the latter. The effect of these changes is to remove counterexamples like that posed by the Rat Man case, but at the cost of making the theory less easily testable. For whereas Freud's theories, until about 1909, required quite definitive events to take place in the child-hood of a neurotic, events that could be witnessed and later recounted by adults, Freud's later theory required no more than psychological events in childhood, events that might well remain utterly private. The changes in the theory, then, resulted in fewer constraints on behavior." (Glymour, *Theory and Evidence*, p. 277)

Under these conditions, we might say that if Freud had indeed learned something in the Rat Man case, his conceptions evolved under the pressure of facts in a direction that tended increasingly to release the psychoana-lytic reconstructions of his patients' past from the obligation of being true in any sense other than "psychological." And this is what Wittgenstein meant when he observed that, in the end, the point is less to reconstruct the real story than to tell and get the patient to accept a story that has the satisfying and soothing character of a plausible myth.

Following Freud himself, a frequent distinction is made between meta-psychology, regarded as a sort of speculative, provisional, unstable, more or less optional superstructure susceptible to being amputated or modi-fied, if need be, without harm to psychoanalysis, and clinical theory, which is itself much closer to experience and based on a multitude of re-peated observations and duly tested inferences concerning the specific facts of mental life. It is the clinical theory and its scientifically proven method that constitute the hard and stable core of psychoanalytic theory. Furthermore, because the distinction between the two parts of the edifice is certainly not as strict as one might imagine, it is understandable why in Wittgenstein's view mythology intrudes, not only on the level of general models of the structure and functioning of the mental apparatus which are introduced to crown the theoretical edifice in some way, but also in the most central concepts of clinical theory itself, for example in the concept of resistance. The speculative nature of metapsychology would cause little concern if it were only what it claims to be, and if the experimental status of the clinical theory really could have been established. Wittgenstein maintains that it has not been and could not be done.

Adolf Grünbaum has harshly criticized two current interpretations of Freudian theory that seem to him to rest on a basic misunderstanding. The first comes from Popper, who maintains that psychoanalysis is in essence irrefutable, and therefore nonscientific. Grünbaum states: "My hunch was that his indictment of the Freudian corpus as inherently untestable had fundamentally misdiagnosed its very genuine epistemic defects, which are often quite subtle."[16] Freud could indeed modify his theories, which he recast at different times in a way that shows he was perfectly capable of assimilating clinical or extraclinical discoveries unfavorable to them. And even if he did not finally manage to resolve the problem of the patient's suggestibility in a satisfying way, nonetheless in different recastings of the theory he entertained and brilliantly discussed this question. In fact, "Freud had carefully addressed—albeit unsuccessfully—all of Popper's arguments against clinical validation well before Popper appeared on the philosophic scene" (*Foundations of Psychoanalysis*, p. 285). Grünbaum's answer to the question of the respectability of psychoanalysis as a presumed scientific enterprise is, in the end, hardly less negative than Popper's; but Popper's reasons are not the right ones. Against Popper, Grünbaum maintains that Freud was in fact a good falsificationist, always careful to safeguard the falsifiability of the analyst's reconstructions of the patient's past.

The second interpretation Grünbaum rejects is what might be called the "hermeneutic" interpretation (Paul Ricoeur, Jürgen Habermas), which maintains that the status of psychoanalysis, contrary to what Freud suggests, is quite different from that of a natural science (and perhaps of any science at all), and that the notion of causality (such as it is) in the dynamic of psychoanalytic therapy cannot be the one Freud had in mind when he compares the case of psychoanalysis to that of a discipline like physics. Since Wittgenstein, for his own reasons, does not believe that psychoanalytic technique can clarify hidden causal connections or that psychoanalysis can be regarded as a causal discipline, he might perhaps be accused, *mutatus mutandis*, of the same kind of incomprehension as Ricoeur and Habermas, and in general all the defenders of what Grünbaum calls the "*acausal* hermeneutic." But curiously, Wittgenstein is cited only once in the book (ibid., p. 60). Grünbaum reckons that "by abjuring causal claims, the radical hermeneutician forsakes not only the etiologic rationale for the presumed therapeuticity of lifting repressions, but also the causal attribution of such therapeutic efficacy. On this account, why should any troubled patient go to an analyst at all?" (ibid., p. 60). If we take it as far as the complete absence of causality, this "rationalization without causation" threatens to deprive us in the end not only of rational intelligibility but also of the causal explicability of the therapeutic effect of the process which the psychoanalytic cure is supposed to induce.

Grünbaum recalls that in the "Preliminary Communication" introducing their *Studies on Hysteria*, Breuer and Freud drew the decisive conclusion that became the pillar of the clinical theory of repression, formulating the etiologic hypothesis that "in the pathogenesis of a psychoneurosis repression plays the generic causal role of a *sine qua non*" (p. 10). After noting that the therapeutic benefits obtained by their method of treatment could be attributed causally to the cathartic recuperation of repressed traumatic memories, they tried to explain this therapeutic efficacy by showing that the desired explanation could be deduced from "the etiologic postulate that repression is causally necessary not only for the initial development of a neurotic disorder but also for its maintenance." (ibid., p. 11). From their observations Breuer and Freud drew the conclusion that the causal connection between the psychic trauma at the origin of the trouble and the hysterical phenomenon was not that of an "agent provocateur" in releasing a symptom, which thereafter leads an independent existence; rather the psychic trauma, or the memory of the trauma, acts like a foreign body which, long after its entry into the mental world of the patient, still demonstrates its presence and its impact through the production of determined effects (cf. *Studies on Hysteria*, p. 6). The main foundation of therapeutic efficacy, then, can be formulated as follows:

> We may reverse the dictum "*cessante causa cessat effectus*" ["when the cause ceases the effect ceases"] and conclude from these observations that the determining process continues to operate in some way or other for years—not indirectly, through a chain of intermediate causal links, but as a *directly* releasing cause—just as a psychical pain that is remembered in waking consciousness still provokes a lachrymal secretion long after the event. *Hysterics suffer mainly from reminiscences.* (ibid., p. 7)

This causal connection is what guarantees that the elimination of the pathogenic cause will result in the disappearance of the illness. And as Grünbaum remarks (*Foundations of Psychoanalysis*, p. 12), the patient is supposed to obtain the sought-for therapeutic benefit by *making use* of the causal connection in question, and not, as Habermas would have it, by "overcoming" or "dissolving" some connection of this kind through the power of reflection.

The therapeutic efficacy of the method of treatment Freud refined in the following years can be similarly explained only on condition that the analyst's interpretation of the psychic material during the cure leads sooner or later to the identification of pathogenic elements that were activated at a particular moment in the history of the patient's mental life and still operate in a truly causal way. The weak point in Wittgenstein's critique of Freud might be, then, his characteristic tendency to concentrate only on the problem of interpretation and the particular "charm" of, say, interpretations that allude to sexuality in general and more specifically to episodes of a sexual nature that intervened or supposedly intervened in early childhood. Wittgenstein seems to discount the various arguments Freud invokes in favor of the existence of the pathogenic role of factors and episodes of this kind, to which we must, he says, attribute direct causal action on the psychic life of the individual as an adult. The problem is, however, that any "historic" and causal hypotheses the psychoanalyst formulates with regard to the infantile sexual life of his patients can hardly be confirmed except by the interested adults, and while it is clearly difficult for them to refute these hypotheses, they may have reasons for accepting them that, in Wittgenstein's view, do not necessarily have much to do with their truth. As Cioffi remarks, "It has not generally been realized how often Freud implies (what his practice confirms) that the character of a child's infantile sexual life is to be determined by waiting until he is an adult and then psychoanalyzing him" ("Wittgenstein's Freud," p. 207). The retrospective "discoveries" that can then be made have in their favor the concurrence of the interested party and the resulting therapeutic benefit (for reasons we don't really understand); but ordinarily we would not consider this sufficient proof of the reality of the events and of the presumed processes. Kraus writes: "Science formerly refused to recognize the sexual drive of adults. The new science concedes that the infant already experiences sexual pleasure during defecation. The old concept was better. For it was at least contradicted by certain declarations of the interested parties."[17] The new theory has the advantage over the old one of being impervious to the denials of adults and even confirmed by the approbation they are likely to give to a historic reconstruction, in which the possibilities of effective verification are essentially what transpires, in the context of the cure, between the analyst and the patient. Even if Wittgenstein's remarks are not adequate to settle the question altogether, they at least have the merit of drawing our attention to the fact that it is the interpretation itself, and the reactions it evokes in the patient in the course of treatment, that constitute the primary thing. As Cioffi says:

> "The behavior of patients under analysis, which began as evidence of the vicissitudes through which they had passed, gradually became criteria for the ascription of these vicissitudes. To say of a patient that he had entertained such and such wishes, or had repressed such and such phantasies, is to say that he now behaves towards the analyst in such and such a way, responds to the proffered interpretations in such and such a manner. Interpretation has been dehistoricized. The notion of truthfulness has replaced that of truth. The narration of infantile reminiscences has been assimilated (incoherently) to the narration of dreams." ("Wittgenstein's Freud," p. 208)

Freud abandoned the seduction theory when he realized that the episodes of sexual violence his patients claimed to have experienced in childhood, the basis of his whole theory of hysteria, had in reality in most cases never taken place and were, in fact, simply the products of their imagination. (Let us note, however, that although the abandonment of the seduction theory seems to imply for some of his critics the decision to entirely ignore "material reality" in favor of "psychic reality," which is, as he says, the reality of the neurosis, Freud continued to admit that seduction by adults was an attested reality, and that it could indeed have taken place in certain cases and constituted the cause of the observed difficulties (cf. for example, *Introductory Lectures*, lecture 23). Jeffrey Masson, in a book that has provoked violent polemics, maintains that the position Freud adopted when he renounced the seduction theory led to a disastrous indifference toward the reality of the traumatic events assumed to be at the source of the patient's difficulties: "Freud is saying that whether seduction actually took place or was only a fantasy does not matter. What matters, for Freud, are the psychological effects, and these effects, Freud states, are no different where the event is a real one or imagined. But in actuality there is an essential difference between the effects of an act that took place and one that was imagined."[18] Ferenczi will try in vain to remind Freud in 1932 that "people fall ill because of what happened to them, and not because of what they imagined happened to them" (Masson, *The Assault on Truth*, p. 186). Masson's conclusion could not be clearer:

> The *Studies on Hysteria* and *The Interpretation of Dreams* are revolutionary books in ways that no subsequent book written by Freud would be. True, he enabled people to speak about their sexual lives in ways that were impossible before his writings. But by shifting the emphasis from an actual world of sadness, misery, and cruelty to an internal stage on which actors performed invented dramas for an invisible audience of their own creations, Freud began a trend away from the real world that, it seems to me, is at the root of the present-day sterility of psychoanalysis and psychiatry throughout the world. (ibid., p. 144)

Clearly, even if the memory of an imaginary event is psychically as real as the memory of an event that actually took place, and can from a causal point of view have the same effects, the much greater malleability of psychic reality and its extreme vulnerability to suggestion must create the disagreeable impression that at this point Freud resigned himself to a considerably weakened case, which nonetheless had some decided advantages in his initial theoretical construction. Whether or not Masson's account is accurate, the unfortunate episode of the seduction theory would tend, it seems, to confirm the final predominance of the element Allan Janik calls "mythopoetic" over the properly scientific aspect of Freudian theory, thus justifying the Austrian critics of psychoanalysis (notably, but not only, Wittgenstein). If Masson is right, when Freud found himself constrained to abandon the "scientific fairy tale" (Krafft-Ebing's expression) represented by the (real) seduction theory, he replaced it with another which was, if not more true to life, in any case more acceptable to the scientific community (what Janik calls the "metaphysical edifice of the Oedipus complex"). Janik judges that:

> If there is anything valid in Masson's thesis, it certainly brings aid and comfort to the critics of psychoanalysis, for whom Freud's would-be science represents a therapeutic myth that has been more or less successful. It must be said that the converse is also true, that the conceptual particularities of the kind that Ebner, Wittgenstein, and Schnitzler specifically refer to apropos psychoanalysis tend to confirm, not the facts on which Masson bases his demonstration, but the *plausibility* of his general position.[19]

It seems to me, however, that Grünbaum is entirely right when he observes (*Foundations of Psychoanalysis*, p. 50) that if a real etiological connection exists between the memories of imaginary sexual episodes and hysteria, this connection is certainly not impugned by the discovery of the fictitious nature of the episodes in question, and that the causal role played by memories of imagined events must be established, as with memories of real events, by the same methods we generally use to establish the existence of a causal connection. In other words, the crucial question is and remains whether or not Freud employed appropriate methods to discover the causes he sought and to justify his causal assertions. And unfortunately, Grünbaum does not believe this to be the case: "Just as the method of free association is incompetent to warrant the pathogenicity of truly occurring childhood seductions, so also this method cannot attest that imagined ones were etiologic" (ibid.).

In his discussion of the fundamental principles of Freudian methodology, Grünbaum grants central importance to an argument that Freud formulated in 1917 and was then obliged to abandon, a crucial argument that has been, according to Grünbaum, neglected by nearly all the commentators and critics of Freud. In the *Introductory Lectures*, observing that the patient could indeed be led by the doctor during the cure to accept an erroneous hypothesis or theory, but that this would only influence his intellect and certainly not his illness, Freud emphasizes that: "After all, his conflicts will only be successfully solved and his resistances overcome if the anticipatory ideas (*Erwartungsvorstellungen*) he is given tally with what is real in him. Whatever in the doctor's conjectures is inaccurate drops out in the course of the analysis; it has to be withdrawn and replaced by something more correct" (*Introductory Lectures*, lecture 28, "Analytic Therapy," p. 452). It is on this argument, which Grünbaum calls the "Tally Argument," that Freud based the "sovereign, condescending serenity" (*Foundations of Psychoanalysis*, p. 170) with which he usually treats the objection that the patient's supposed self-knowledge, considered a necessary condition for the cure, might really be just the product of the analyst's suggestion. Freud means that the therapeutic effect would not be therapeutic if the "revelations" made possible by the application of analytic technique were simply accepted, for one reason or another, as true by the interested party: they must also *be* true, or at least close enough to the truth. In other words, simple belief (persuasion) is not enough, only the truth itself has the power to bring about the cure.

Grünbaum interprets the passage from the *Introductory Lectures* cited above as affirming that the patient's specific knowledge of his own situation obtained in the course of analysis is *causally necessary* to the cure of his psychoneurosis. The necessary condition thesis (NCT) entails "not only that there is no spontaneous remission of psychoneuroses but also that, if there are any cures at all, psychoanalysis is *uniquely* therapeutic for such disorders as compared to any *rival* therapies" (ibid., p. 140). As it is reconstructed by Grünbaum, the Tally Argument involves two claims or premises of causally necessary conditions, and two conclusions:

> PREMISE 1: Only the psychoanalytic method of interpretation and treatment can yield or mediate to the patient correct insight into the unconscious pathogens of his psychoneurosis, and
>
> PREMISE 2: The analysand's correct insight into the etiology of his affliction and into the unconscious dynamics of his character is, in turn, *causally necessary* for the therapeutic conquest of his neurosis. . . .
>
> CONCLUSION 1: The psychoanalytic interpretations of the hidden causes of P's behavior given to him by his analyst are indeed correct, and thus—as Freud put it—these interpretations "tally with what is real" in P.
>
> CONCLUSION 2: Only analytic treatment could have wrought the conquest of P's psychoneurosis. (cf. ibid., pp. 139–40)

Freud reminds us that "the relationship between analyst and patient is based on a love of truth, that is, on the acknowledgment of reality, and that it precludes any kind of sham or deception" ("Analysis, Terminable and Interminable," pp. 351–52). His confidence in the capacity of his method to reveal things that "tally with reality," whatever the opinion of the interested party on this point, leads him to make declarations like the following: "The path that starts from the analyst's construction ought to end in the patient's recollection; but it does not always lead so far. Quite often we do not succeed in bringing the patient to recollect what has been repressed. Instead of that, if the analysis is carried out correctly, we produce in him an assured conviction of the truth of the construction, which achieves the same therapeutic result as a recaptured memory" ("Construction in Analysis," p. 368). This is the same kind of conviction that leads him at times to present facts that have been made accessible only by analytic interpretation as if they were themselves directly remembered in the process and confirmed; and to declare, for example, that the dream itself is another form of recollection, which might give a malicious reader the impression that the patient's effective amnesia, which in principle constitutes the goal of the analysis, is after all something the analyst can easily bypass.[20] The fact that infantile scenes may not always be consciously remembered does not mean that they are not remembered in another way:

> I am not of the opinion, however, that such scenes must necessarily be phantasies because they do not reappear in the shape of recollections. It seems to me absolutely equivalent to a recollection if the memories are replaced (as in the present case) by dreams, the analysis of which invariably leads back to the same scene, and which reproduce every portion of its content in an indefatigable variety of new shapes. Indeed, dreaming is another kind of remembering, though one that is subject to the conditions that rule at night and the laws of dream formation. It is this recurrence in dreams that I regard as the explanation of the fact that patients themselves gradually acquire a profound conviction of the reality of these primal scenes, a conviction which is in no respect inferior to one based upon recollection." (*From the History of an Infantile Neurosis, CP* 3:524).

The proposal to treat dreams as in some sense "night memories" constitutes another typical example of what Wittgenstein would call an extension of the concept, as it happens the concept of memory, which Freud tends to present as a discovery. According to Grünbaum, the critics who found eminently suspect assertions like those just cited have mistakenly forgotten that, at least at a certain period, Freud thought he had a decisive argument in answer to their objections.

If the Tally Argument had been really conclusive, it would have endorsed the statement that "psychoanalytic treatment successes as a whole vouch for the truth of the Freudian theory of personality, including its specific etiologies of the psychoneuroses and even its general theory of psychosexual development" (*Foundations of Psychoanalysis*, pp. 140–41). And it would have had as a corollary that the psychoanalytic method "has the extraordinary capacity to validate major causal claims by essentially retrospective inquiries, *without* the burdens of prospective longitudinal studies employing (experimental) controls. Yet these causal inferences are not vitiated by *post hoc ergo propter hoc* or other known pitfalls of causal inference" (ibid., p. 141). Naturally, such a conclusion would be fatal for all interpretations which, like Wittgenstein's, contest the notion that Freud succeeded in refining an unprecedented and absolutely unique method for seeking and discovering causes. But Grünbaum himself does not think that Freud ever managed to give the Tally Argument a really convincing form, and he thinks, moreover, that Freud was obliged to reconsider it, beginning in 1926, and abandoned it in the end because he realized that its two causal premises, which he had regarded for decades as empirically justified, were placed in serious jeopardy by the existence of spontaneous remissions, on the one hand, and on the other by the quality and precariousness of the therapeutic results obtained by psychoanalytic treatment (cf. ibid., p. 160).

I am not at all certain myself that the above-mentioned crucial passage from the *Introductory Lectures* really was an "audacious declaration" of the thesis of causal necessity. It seems to me more reasonable to suppose that Freud is simply responding here, as he does on other occasions, to the objection that invokes the patient's suggestibility, observing more modestly that if the analyst's suggestions did not correspond with the *facts*, the patient's conflicts would not be resolved and his resistances suppressed; this does not imply, it seems to me, any direct effect on the possible success or failure of methods of treatment other than psychoanalysis. Whatever the case, the Tally Argument perhaps proves that Freud was, as Grünbaum would have it, a much more aware and incomparably more sophisticated epistemologist than even his most sympathetic critics have recognized. As Grünbaum himself admits, however, it would not constitute—and this is really the main point—an adequate response to the causal skepticism of critics like Wittgenstein, even if this skepticism required more extensive argumentation than Wittgenstein himself had occasion, or was perhaps able, to provide.

The least we can say is that Freud's final position on the reality of infantile scenes conjured from the patient's memory during analysis is neither very clear nor very satisfying. In the analysis of the Wolf Man case, he says that the primal scene involves "the picture of sexual intercourse between the boy's parents in an attitude especially favorable to certain observations":

> Let us assume as an uncontradicted premise that a primal scene of this kind has been correctly evolved technically, that it is indispensable to a comprehensive solution of all the conundrums that are set us by the symptoms of the infantile disorder, that all the consequences radiate out from it, just as all the threads of the analysis have led up to it. Then, in view of its content, it is impossible that it can be anything else than the reproduction of a reality experienced by the child. For a child, like an adult, can produce phantasies only from material which has been acquired from some source or other; and with children some of the means of acquiring it (by reading, for instance) are cut off, while the space of time at their disposal for acquiring it is short and can easily be searched with a view to the discovery of such sources. (*From the History of an Infantile Neurosis, CP* 3:528)

Yet, while he opposes the theory that holds infantile scenes to be nothing but regressive fantasies, Freud admits that they may well be such without this changing the problem the analyst must solve or his way of treating it: "The analysis would have to run precisely the same course as one which had a *naif* faith in the truth of the phantasies. The difference would only come at the end of the analysis, after the phantasies had been laid bare" (ibid., *CP* 3:522). It would therefore be indispensable, in any event, if only to obtain the cooperation of the patient, to act *as if* these fantasies corresponded to real events. Finally, Freud admits that knowing whether or not the fantasies in question have an objective value is not really important:

> I should myself be glad to know whether the primal scene in my present patient's case was a phantasy or a real experience; but, taking other similar cases into account, I must admit that the answer to this question is not in reality a matter of very great importance. These scenes of observing parental intercourse, of being seduced in childhood, and of being threatened with castration are unquestionably an inherited endowment, a phylogenetic inheritance, but they may just as easily be acquired by personal experience. With my patient, his seduction by his elder sister was an indisputable reality; why should not the same have been true of his observation of his parents' intercourse?
>
> All that we find in the prehistory of neuroses is that a child catches hold of this phylogenetic experience where his own experience fails him. He fills in the gaps in individual truth with prehistoric truth; he replaces occurrences in his own life by occurrences in the life of his ancestors." (*ibid.*, viii: "Material from the Primal Period—Solution," p. 577)

> The impression we gain is that these events of childhood are somehow demanded as a necessity, that they are among the essential elements of a neurosis. If they have occurred in reality, so much to the good; but if they have been withheld by reality, they are supplemented by phantasy. The outcome is the same, and up to the present we have not succeeded in pointing to any difference in the consequences, whether phantasy or reality has had the greater share in these events of childhood. (*Introductory Lectures*, p. 390)

In other words, it is always possible, if need be, to replace the acquired recollection of an event that really happened in the life of an individual by the recollection, imprinted in the memory of the species, of events that surely happened at some distant period in its history. The second kind of recollection can assume exactly the same etiological role as the first. The inconvenience of this supposition is that it becomes at once almost useless to try and really test the interpretation in relation to the facts of the individual history, whose reality is most often impossible to establish with certainty and will always be suspect. It is therefore difficult not to conclude, as Cioffi does, that "with phylogenetic inheritance to fall back on Freud deprives himself of any way of discovering that his reconstructions are mistaken and his principles of interpretation invalid, which means that he deprives himself of any reason for believing that they are not" ("Wittgenstein's Freud," pp. 202–203).

But it is not really very important whether Freud's reconstructions are true or false if, as Wittgenstein believes, they are basically accepted because of their enormous charm, received spontaneously as explanations that *must be* true and not as hypotheses whose truth or falseness is crucial. The events they relate, like those in myths, are events that *had to* happen, and not events whose actual occurrence is at issue. The question of their historical reality is perhaps impossible to resolve, but it is stripped of any real relevance. If Wittgenstein had been able to read the passages just cited, he would only have found in them additional confirmation of his idea that the relief brought by the "historical" explanations proposed by psychoanalysis is comparable to the relief procured by narratives that link the most problematic aspects and episodes in the life of the individual to mythic events which occurred at some distant era in the life of the species. What is satisfying in these explanations is primarily the necessity and tragic character they confer on events that seem at first glance completely bereft of these elements:

> Freud refers to various ancient myths in these connexions, and claims that his researches have now explained how it came about that anybody should think or propound a myth of that sort. Whereas in fact Freud has done something different. He has not given a scientific explanation of the ancient myth. What he has done is to propound a new myth. The attractiveness of the suggestion, for instance, that all anxiety is a repetition of the anxiety of the birth trauma, is just the attractiveness of mythology. "It is all the outcome of something that happened long ago." Almost like referring to a totem.
>
> Much the same could be said of the notion of an "Urszene." This often has the attractiveness of giving a sort of tragic pattern to one's life. It is all the repetition of the same pattern which was settled long ago. Like a tragic figure carrying out the decrees under which the fates had placed him at birth. Many people have, at some period, serious trouble in their lives—so serious as to lead to thoughts of suicide. This is likely to appear to one as something nasty, as a situation which is too foul to be a subject of a tragedy. And it may then be an immense relief if it can be shown that one's life has the pattern rather of a tragedy—the tragic working out and repetition of a pattern which was determined by the primal scene.
>
> There is of course the difficulty of determining what scene is the primal scene—whether it is the scene which the patient recognizes as such, or whether it is the one whose recollection effects the cure. In practice these criteria are mingled together. (*Lectures and Conversations*, p. 51)

CHAPTER IV

Reasons and Causes

Psychology belongs to the ratioide realm, and the multiplicity of its facts is not infinite, as the possibility of psychology as an empirical science teaches. The only things that have boundless diversity are psychic *motives*, and psychology has nothing to do with these.

—ROBERT MUSIL, *Skizze der Erkenntnis des Dichters* (1918)

MOORE REPORTS Wittgenstein as saying that the initial confusion of *cause* and *reason* had led to the disciples of Freud making an "abominable mess" ("Wittgenstein's Lectures in 1930–33," p. 316). In *The Blue Book*, Wittgenstein explains his point on the difference Freud is accused of neglecting:

> The proposition that your action has such and such a cause, is a hypothesis. The hypothesis is well-founded if one has had a number of experiences which, roughly speaking, agree in showing that your action is the regular sequel of certain conditions which we then call causes of the action. In order to know the reason which you had for making a certain statement, for acting in a particular way, etc., no number of agreeing experiences is necessary, and the statement of your reason is not a hypothesis. (p. 15)

For event A to be considered the cause of event B, one would have to verify that in a sufficient number of cases events of the A variety are regularly followed by events of the B variety. Of course, an event of the first type could still happen without being followed by an event of the second type. The relation of causation (*Verursachung*) is therefore hypothetical in a sense that the relation between a reason and the action it explains (*Begründung*) is not. A reason is characterized by the capacity to be recognized as such by the person whose reason it is, and not on the basis of an inductive inference. Yet Freud either formulates causal hypotheses, and in this case he must try and verify them by methods different from his own; or he proposes and imposes reasons, and the acceptance of a reason has nothing to do with the acceptance of an explanatory hypothesis of the causal type, or for that matter with any hypothesis at all. During the treatment, of course, the psychoanalyst may be led to propose various reasons in a hypothetical way; he may even be convinced rather soon, sometimes well before the end of the process, that he knows the *true* reason for the analysand's behavior and yet fail in the end, despite his efforts, to get the patient to agree that this was his reason. But Wittgenstein maintains that even a reason that is simply possible is different from a supposed cause, in the sense that it is presented as something the agent might in principle recognize; and when it is accepted, what makes it the reason for the behavior in question is essentially the fact that the interested party recognizes it as such.

In fact, the situation is more complicated than it might initially seem, since it is difficult, for example, always to subordinate the perception of a causal relation to a repeated experience of the consecutive nature of the two events. Aren't there and don't there have to be cases in which we instantaneously perceive the cause and know it immediately with absolute certainty? In the *Philosophical Investigations*, after evoking the idea that in reading we experience internally a kind of causality of signs which we see in the words we utter, Wittgenstein adds:

> But why do you say that we felt a causal connexion? Causation is surely something established by experiments, by observing a regular concomitance of events for example. So how could I say that I *felt* something which is established by experiment? (It is indeed true that observation of regular concomitances is not the only way we establish causation.) One might rather say, I feel that the letters are the *reason* why I read such-and-such. For if someone asks me "Why do you read such-and-such?"—I justify my reading by the letters which are there. (sec. 169)

In a manuscript from 1937 on cause and effect, Wittgenstein wonders if one can say, as Russell was saying, that cause is known by intuition before being known by the repetition of experiments. And he admits that an experience exists that might be called an "experience of the cause" (we know immediately that pain follows a blow), "but not because it infallibly shows us the cause, but because in seeking the cause we have *one* root of the language game of cause and effect."[1] The language game of the determination of causes could not exist if its source was not an instinctive behavior consistent with seeking the cause and seeking to suppress the effect by suppressing the cause:

> "*We react to the cause.*
> Calling something "cause" is analogous to showing and saying: "That is *his* fault!"

> We instinctively push away the cause when we do not want the effect. We instinctively look from the person who is struck to the one who strikes. (I am assuming that we do this.) ("Ursache und Wirkung," p. 392; cf. p. 399)

Even taking account of this important qualification, the language game of seeking causes is nonetheless basically different in grammatical terms from the language game of seeking reasons or justifications. Wittgenstein as usual pushes aside the possibility of considering as a secondary difference the fact that reasons and causes are never discovered and recognized in the same way. And as we have already had occasion to realize at the outset, he considers that the worst way of trying to reconstruct the lost unity would be to consider reasons as "felt" causes, causes experienced internally. He explicitly rejects, then, the theory defended by Schopenhauer, according to which: *"Motivation is causality seen from within.* As a result, causality presents itself here in a totally different way, in a totally different setting, for a totally different kind of knowledge: this is why it must now be introduced as a particular and specific form of our proposition, which seems from this fact like a *principle of sufficient reason for the action*, principium rationis sufficientis agendi, in short, *the law of motivation"* (*On the Basis of Morality*, sec. 43). Schopenhauer maintains that motivation is only "causality passing through knowledge," and that the motive operates with the same necessity as all causes. The law of motivation, like the law of causality, is a natural law and it is applied with the same rigor:

> Insofar as man is a part of nature, the *human will* certainly also has a *law*, and indeed this law is strictly demonstrable, inviolable, without exception, firm as a rock, and does not, like the categorical imperative, imply a *quasi* but a *real* necessity. It is the *law* of motivation, a form of the law of causality, namely, causality brought about through the medium of knowledge. This is the only demonstrable law to which the human will *as such* is subject. It states that every action can take place only in consequence of a sufficient motive. Like the law of causality generally, it is a natural law.[2]

In other words, the fact that knowledge is the necessary medium for the causality of motives does not prevent the law of motivation from being simply a special instance of the law of causality, and of bowing to an equally strict determinism. Wittgenstein regards this as a grammatical confusion. For him, the causal connection is simply not the sort of thing that might be the subject, on the one hand, of a hypothesis and, on the other, of an immediate experience. As he says in one of his manuscripts: "The 'causal connexion' is not a primary connexion, nor does this mean, then, that it can be felt (or other things of this sort)."

Interestingly, however, Wittgenstein himself sometimes typically vacillates (like everyone) between the language of reasons and the language of causes, and although he thinks that psychoanalysis is not a causal discipline and that it discovers reasons, not causes, he nonetheless writes in the *Philosophical Investigations*:

> I can at first give no answer to the question *why* I imagine the city in *this* direction. I had *no reason* to think it. But though I see no reason still I seem to see certain psychological causes for it. In particular, certain associations and memories. For example, we walked along a canal, and once before in similar circumstances I had followed a canal and that time the city lay on our right.—I might try as it were psychoanalytically to discover the causes of my unfounded conviction. (p. 215e).

Wittgenstein speaks here of the possibility of using a method analogous to psychoanalysis to reconstruct the causal train of associations, recollections, etc., that led to the unjustified conviction whose source I am trying to determine. Nonetheless, the psychoanalyst who explains a dream, a slip, or a parapraxis is not giving a causal explanation, in Wittgenstein's view.

We can say, if we like, that one cannot know a cause but only conjecture it; by contrast, a reason is by nature something that can be known, and is only conjectured in a provisional way and with the view to possible recognition (we are speaking, of course, of a logical possibility, not a practical one) by the interested party:

> Of the cause one can say that one can't *know* it but can only *conjecture* it. On the other hand, one often says: "Surely *I* must know why I did it" talking of the *motive*. When I say: "We can only *conjecture* the cause but we *know* the motive" this statement will be seen later on to be a grammatical one. The "can" refers to a *logical* possibility. (*The Blue Book*, p. 15)

The fact that the subject is generally unaware of a good many of the reasons that make him act does not transform these reasons into causes, hence hypotheses. What he is unaware of in such a case are precisely reasons, not causes. In other words, Freud treats the reason for an action like a cause by supposing that it can be conjectured by a scientific sort of procedure and confirmed in the end by the acquiescence of the subject, who recognizes it as having indeed been his reason; and he treats the cause like a reason by supposing that the causes he seeks can be known in the second way, which has nothing to do with the way causal hypotheses are verified in an experimental science.

Cioffi wondered whether, in speaking of a confusion between reasons and causes, we are not leaving out an essential element: reasons which are causes do indeed constitute reasons which the subject may very well be unaware of (as he is unaware of most causes of his behavior) or fail to accept, despite the fact that they are indeed the "true" reasons (according to the theory). To say that the action was determined by an unconscious process amounts to saying that it was produced by something that can be both unperceived and remain so (like a cause) and known with immediate certainty (like a reason); so it is always possible to interpret the subject's refusal as a normal (but inconsequential) disagreement over the cause of his action, and his assent as proof of the fact that the true reason was really identified:

> The objection to speaking in this connexion of the "abominable mess" made by Freud's disciples in confusing cause and reason is that it represents the state of affairs too much as one of helpless confusion and overlooks the way in which the confusion is ingeniously exploited in the interests of the theory. In the notion of reasons which are causes there is more grammatical flair than grammatical muddle. ("Wittgenstein's Freud," p. 195)

It is sometimes assumed that reasons do not easily fall into the category of causes because causes act automatically and restrictively, while reasons act in a way that is, or should be compatible with, the exercise of free will. We might say that in contrast to causes, reasons bend without forcing. Once we know a cause, all other things being equal, the usual effect inevitably follows. Nothing like this can be said of reasons. A sufficient reason for one person in certain circumstances is not necessarily the same for another, nor for the same person in different circumstances. For a reason to act like a determining cause of action depends on a multitude of various conditions which are a priori difficult, if not impossible, to determine. If reasons are causes, they are causes which act in a way that does not lend itself to the formulation of causal laws. One of the major advantages of motivational explanation over causal explanation is precisely that the explanatory power of a motive is not subordinated to the existence of an invariable connection between the motive and the behavior it explains.

But Wittgenstein is the first to observe that a law is simply the expression of a natural regularity, and that it is an illusion to imagine that a law in any way forces events to unfold as they do: "What on earth would it mean that natural law compels a thing to go as it goes? The natural law is correct and that's all. There is no reason why, even if there was regularity in human decisions, I should not be free. There is nothing about regularity which makes anything free or not free. The notion of compulsion is there if you think of the regularity as compelled; as produced by rails. If, besides the notion of regularity, you bring in the notion of: 'It must move like this because the rails are laid like this.' "[3] Wittgenstein calls our attention to the fact that the explanation by causes and the explanation by reasons correspond to two different language games. Nothing he says suggests that he is also prepared to defend the incompatibility of these different explanations.

It is often supposed that if a behavior could be cogently explained by its causes, it would seem determined in a way that leaves no room for things like intentions, deliberations, reasons, or motives, and the intentional explanation of the action would then lose its justification and meaning. Wittgenstein simply does not think this is so. Even a strictly deterministic explanation of the course of human events, if it could be given, would not necessarily dissuade us from adopting the attitude (for it is chiefly a matter of attitude) that involves imputing reasons and assigning responsibilities:

> We know how we use such expressions as "responsible," "free," and "can't help it," etc. Now the uses of these expressions are quite independent of whether or not there are laws of nature. . . . Holding oneself responsible, holding another responsible—these are attitudes. So the attitude one takes toward a drunk—praising—blaming—is different from what we take toward a sober man who may do what the drunk does. (Bouwsma, *Conversations, 1949–1951*)

A demonstration of the truth of determinism as a theory, if we could imagine such a thing, would perhaps have no effect on this reaction.

The important "logical" difference between *Begründung* and *Verursachung* and between reasons and causes must not, then, be sought in this direction; and, as we have seen, this is not where Wittgenstein seeks it. Even if an action was done "mechanically" or "automatically," I may still be capable of giving a reason for it after the fact, if I am asked for one (by indicating a rule, for example, or showing a paradigm) (cf. *The Blue Book*, p. 14). And this does not make the explanation by reason any more analogous to the explanation by cause. The point is not the somewhat mythic inexorability of causes and the supposed tolerance of reasons. As Dennett notes, explanations that we can generally call "intentional" (meaning simply that they invoke thoughts, desires, beliefs, knowledge, intentions, etc., but certainly not that they attribute the conscious possession of these to the subject of the action) are perhaps, among other things, causal explanations, but they "are at least not causal explanations *simpliciter*" (*Brainstorms*, p. 235) Dennett demonstrates this by contrasting authentically intentional explanations with "causal hybrids" of the following type:

1. His belief that the gun was loaded caused his heart attack.
2. His obsessive desire for revenge caused his ulcers.
3. The thought of his narrow escape from the rattler made him shudder.

These explanations, though they invoke a desire, a belief, or another intentional phenomenon, betray their "Humean" nature, according to Dennett, by being subject to the usual rules of evidence for causal assertions. Wittgenstein would say that, strictly speaking, they indicate a cause and not a reason for the event, the state, or the action. Properly intentional explanations have the effect of giving a rationale for the *explicandum*, explaining a behavior or an action "by making it reasonable in the light of certain beliefs, intentions, desires ascribed to the agent" (ibid., p. 236). As do the following statements:

4. He threw himself to the floor because of his belief that the gun was loaded.
5. His obsessive desire for revenge led him to follow Jones all the way to Burma.
6. He refused to pick up the snake because at that moment he thought of his narrow escape from the rattler. (ibid.)

As Dennett says:

> The difference in what one is attempting to provide in mechanistic and intentional explanations is especially clear in the case of "psychosomatic" disorders. One can say—in the manner of (1) and (2)—that a desire or belief merely *caused* a symptom, say, paralysis, or one can say that a desire or belief led a person to *want* to be paralyzed—to become paralyzed *deliberately*. The latter presumes to be a purely intentional explanation, a case of making the paralysis—as an *intended condition*—*reasonable* in the light of certain beliefs and desires, e.g., the desire to be waited on, the belief that relatives must be made to feel guilty. (ibid.)

Even if the desire or belief must have had an impact that could be qualified as causal in the second case as well as the first, this does not reduce the difference, he thinks, between the instances in which they are invoked simply as causes of the action and those in which they are invoked as reasons that explain it intentionally.

We can say in principle that someone who accepts a reason accepts along with it, at least in some cases, a certain type of causal explanation for his behavior. Donald Davidson has tried to rehabilitate the traditional and usual position, which holds that rationalizing an action is a particular kind of causal explanation.[4] In his view, unless we allow that reasons must also be understood as causes, we have no satisfactory explanation of what we mean when we say that "agent X performed the action because he had the reason." In fact, "a reason is a rational cause" ("Psychology as Philosophy," p. 233). The partisans of a very strict distinction between rationalization and causal explanation observe that the relation between a reason and the action it explains is a logical and internal relation, since a reason consists of redescribing the action with the effect of making it intelligible, whereas the relation of cause and effect is an empirical and external relation between two events. To this Davidson objects that nonetheless the redescription of the action also describes it as having been produced by certain causes, and that, correlatively, a true causal statement (in the sense that it really identifies the cause) can be analytic or synthetic depending on the way it describes the cause in question. He would argue that, at least in some cases, determining the real motive of the action amounts to identifying a causal agent which has effectively produced the action.

Wittgenstein, for his part, insists that we cannot say of a reason, as we would of a cause, that the reason is a good one if it predicts with some probability (and perhaps even certainty) the occurrence of the event concerned. To say that a reason is a good reason simply means that it corresponds to a certain standard of the good reason, which isn't necessarily right. What makes a reason we accept the *good* reason is, however, precisely the question we should ask in those cases in which the relation of the reason to the facts it justifies is an empirical relation: "If the justification of a belief were an empirical relation, then we ought to ask again: 'And why is this specifically a reason for that belief?' And so on in this way." We can therefore consider the justification by reason as a relation that experience teaches us without any immediate risk of being led into an infinite regression. It is not experience that justifies us in considering something a (good) reason: "Experience teaches that the cause of B is A, and consequently that A happens is a good reason to suppose that B will happen. But we cannot say that experience teaches that the repeated experience of coincidence is a good reason to suppose that coincidences will continue." And the fact is that when we are asked the reason for a belief, we do not proceed in the same way as when we are asked the cause of an event: "Interrogated on the reasons for a supposition, we reflect on those reasons (*man besinnt sich*). Is this the same process as when we reflect on the possible causes of an event?" In the *Philosophical Investigations*, Wittgenstein invites us to compare the two following language games: (a) a language game in which someone gives someone else an order to make particular movements with his arm, or to assume particular bodily positions; (b) a language game in which someone observes certain regular processes—for example, the reactions of different metals to acids—and thereupon makes predictions about the reactions that will occur in certain cases. He remarks: "There is evident kinship between these two language-games, and also a fundamental difference. In both one might call the spoken words 'predictions.' But compare the training which leads to the first technique with the training for the second one" (sec. 630). Perhaps this is all we can say, after all, about the language games of rational explanations and causal explanations, that they bear the marks of both an evident kinship (the knowledge of reasons can, like that of causes, be used to formulate predictions) and an essential difference (the two language games are not learned or played in the same way).

The grammatical difference Wittgenstein establishes between reasons and causes, and between the explanation by reasons and the explanation by causes, seems to have been mostly understood as meaning that if something is a reason, it cannot simultaneously be a cause. Yet Wittgenstein says nothing that explicitly excludes this possibility; in his *Remarks on the Philosophy of Psychology, 1946–1947*, we find the following statement:

> Giving the motive is a specific language game—just as uttering a wish or an intention, is a specific language game. A dog won't learn to speak, just as a pig won't learn to retrieve. Some men don't learn to speak, some learn some language games, not others—e.g., learn to say "apple" for an apple and never learn "if . . . then" nor yet to give motives.
>
> If I fear something it doesn't mean "I feel jittery, is it his face? Take it away and see if I still feel jittery." Similarly with delight. The expression of fear or delight contains an object. (It is irrelevant that there is also fear "of nothing.") Giving the motive of an action is like stating the object of fear or delight; the motive, or the object, *may* also be a cause.
>
> Must the motive be a *likely cause* of the action? If I say I murdered him because he ate an apple and don't say I wanted the apple or hate people who eat apples, then the other chap won't accept this motive as a likely cause.[5]

The crucial point seems to be that even if the reason or motive can eventually be a cause, it cannot ever be simply a cause. It would be rather excessive, then, to impute to Wittgenstein the claim that the explanation by reasons and the explanation by causes are incompatible. What he does claim is that the first type of explanation is not reducible to the second. Davidson himself recognizes that there is no really satisfying way to determine what kind of cause a reason must be for one to say that it rationalizes the action: "What I despair of spelling out is the way in which attitudes must cause actions if they are to rationalize the action."[6] We can say, as he does in his chapter "Intending," that "an action is performed with a certain intention if it is caused in the right way by attitudes and beliefs that rationalize it."[7] But in the absence of a noncircular definition of "the right way" and of a sufficiently elaborated and plausible version of the claimed causalist reduction, it is difficult to say whether the idea that reasons are causes of an intentional action contains more than the a priori conviction that there *must* be a kind of causality that operates "the right way." There seems to be something intrinsic, on the other hand, that militates against the idea that the reasons for our actions may one day be revealed as simply some possible causes, among others, since this would hardly allow us to preserve the essential distinction between actions we perform and simple things that *happen to us*, for which we disclaim agency.

The explanation by reasons belongs to the category of teleological explanation, which "consists in making phenomena teleologically intelligible rather than predictable from knowledge of their efficient causes."[8] We can say of Freud that he succeeded quite remarkably in extending the realm of teleological explanation by showing that a considerable quantity of mental phenomena and behavior which at first seem to make no sense can indeed be made intelligible in these terms and given an explanation that can be qualified as generally intentional. But Freud himself tends rather to present his accomplishment as extending the methods of causal explanation employed in the natural sciences to a category of phenomena (mental phenomena in general) which had previously seemed impervious to this type of treatment. The intervention of the unconscious is indeed supposed to fill in the gaps of a causal explanation which is inevitably incomplete without our decision to do just this and to explain the perceived by the unperceived, as physicists do. In G. H. von Wright's language we might say that Freud's idea of the "scientific psychology" he is in the process of proposing corresponds to the "Galilean" paradigm much more than to the "Aristotelian" one. The basic difficulty resulting from this situation is well known and has often been remarked. Davidson summarizes it this way: "It seems, then, that there are two irreconcilable tendencies in Freud's methodology. On the one hand he wanted to extend the range of phenomena subject to reason explanations, and on the other to treat these same phenomena as forces and states are treated in the natural sciences. But in the natural sciences, reasons and propositional attitudes are out of place, and blind causality rules."[9] If we accept Davidson's point of view, it seems that Freud might be defended at least on one important point: "There is no inherent conflict between reason explanations and causal explanations. Since beliefs and desires are causes of the actions for which they are reasons, reason explanations include an essential causal element" ("Paradoxes of Irrationality," p. 293). But if we admit that discovering a reason can and even must signify at the same time discovering a (special kind of) cause, what may remain utterly mysterious is the way a cause might be discovered in two ways as radically different from each other as ordinary causes and reasons. As Wittgenstein would say, "from another source of knowledge flows another knowledge" ("Ursache und Wirkung," p. 399).

Friedrich Waismann expresses the difference between causes and motives by saying that a motive is in the nature of an interpretation: "We have drawn attention to the uncertainty of statements having to do with motives and to their capacity to be vulnerable to criticism, and all this suggested the idea that a motive is a sort of *interpretation* that we give to our action; an interpretation that is surely not completely arbitrary, but which strongly depends on the way of 'seeing'." [10] A motive is what makes an action intelligible and endowed with meaning. We might say as well, then, that "a motive is a kind of making sense (*Sinngebung*)" (*Wille und Motiv*, p. 148). The multiplicity of motives is essentially nothing more than the multiplicity of possible interpretations that come to mind when we seek to understand an action. Waismann does not suggest, of course, that motives have no reality and that their discovery has no relation to knowledge, properly speaking. What he means is rather that the psychological vocabulary does not provide us with the appropriate word to designate something which is more than an interpretation yet less than a fact: "I think that one would need a concept that occupies a position midway between three things: cognition (*erkennen*), recognition, (*bekennen*), and interpretation (*deuten*)" (ibid., p. 153). In a paradoxical way, motives are "things that are never completely real and never completely unreal" (ibid., p. 154).

Waismann does not consider, however, that the indication of a motive and the causal explanation are separated by a strict dividing line. Concrete examples help us to realize that the concept of a motive to explain an action tends in some cases to be gradually transformed into the cause of the action, and finally confused with it. The difficulty is that what we ordinarily call a "motive" generally occupies an intermediary position, indecisive and unclassifiable, situated between two seemingly heterogeneous extremes: the reason (what we can recognize, accept, or admit) and the cause (which we can know objectively): "The closer a motive is to a cause, the better it can be known from the outside and governed by laws. The more distant it is from the cause, the more it is referred to self-observation. And this leads us to ask in what sense we can simply speak of the existence of determined motives" (ibid., p. 144). The more motives resemble causes, the more they seem to lend themselves to be formulated as laws of the causal type; the more different they are from causes, the less their action seems subject to causal laws, or to laws of any sort.

All evidence indicates that motives, like causes, are things we can be unaware of and mistaken about. But the question is, how can we be so unaware of them that we are seriously mistaken about what they are? Waismann observes: "A motive is as evanescent as a cloud" (ibid., p. 134). With regard to motivation in general we might formulate an aporia of the following type: If the motive is the cause of the behavior, how is it that at least in some cases we can know it as we do? (This, we might say, is Freud's problem.) It is tempting—and this was done well before Freud—to answer the question how uncertainties and even illusions concerning our own motives are possible by saying that there are unconscious "resistances" which prevent us from penetrating certain aspects of our own psychic interiority, or at least have the effect of deflecting or falsifying our perception of it. This explanation does not satisfy Waismann (or Wittgenstein, as we have noted), for the following reason: "It is not very credible that a force be considered *permanently in operation* that prevents our gaze from penetrating our own interiority; that motives must be entities which lead a kind of self-enclosed existence, which are available in us but which we conceal from ourselves through a more or less circumstantial procedure, through a "censor" or God knows what. We ought rather to face head on the more radical question—*are there simply motives?*" (ibid., pp. 135–36). The more the motive resembles a cause that precedes the action and could act surreptitiously, unknown to us, the more the realism of motives seems a plausible doctrine; on the other hand, the more the motive emerges as an interpretation of the action given after the fact, the more difficult it seems to conceive of motives as entities endowed with a real existence and which may simply, for one reason or another, go unperceived.

Although the model Freud has in mind is clearly that of classical, deterministic, and realistic physics, Waismann suggests that we apply to the psychology of motives some of the considerations that quantum physics has made familiar to us:

> The [uncertainty principle] is not a curtain that veils the most delicate processes from us; it is merely the expression of the fact that we seek to describe atomic processes with an image that just cannot be used. I would now like to propose applying an analogous idea to motives. Given the fact that when one is in search of a motive one never, it seems, arrives at unassailable facts of consciousness, that the motives are usually rather insubstantial and, upon critical scrutiny, slip between our fingers, it is better from the outset not to conceive of them as things that exist in a determined way but rather to look at what really happens when one acts and then formulate for oneself judgments on one's own action." (ibid., p. 139)

The conclusion seems to be that there cannot be a positive science of motivation, as Freud evidently believes, but only at best a hermeneutics. Psychoanalysis indeed exploits the uncertainty and indeterminacy of motives and their inherent tendency to bend to criticism to persuade the subjects that their motives are very different from what they had previously believed. But only the confusion of reasons and causes, and the fact that reasons were previously unperceived, allow any assertion that the realm of objective knowledge has been extended to the universe of reasons. Waismann observes that it is probably not accidental that the word designating pictorial (or musical) *motifs* is related to the word designating the *motives* of human action. This use of the same—or the related—term can be understood better if we think that studying the motive of an action means "seeing the action in its natural environment, integrated within a context of thoughts (whether these are clear or only half formed), desires, aspirations, flights of imagination, dreams, voluntary impulses, inclinations, orientations of interest, etc." (ibid., p. 150). Doubtless such groupings appear in the form of characteristic constellations that endlessly recur and which we call jealousy, hatred, vanity, curiosity, desire to know, adventurous instinct, etc. But there is no fundamental difference between this process and the way the painter makes meaningful regroupings on canvas, understands recurrent "motifs," and brings out characteristic configurations in the landscape he is looking at. In other words, in the language of Wittgenstein, the exploration of motives on the whole invokes the "aesthetic" explanation in the larger sense rather than the causal explanation properly speaking. The fact that psychoanalysis deals basically with motives that are supposed to act from a distance like causes is what gives the impression that access to a world independent of motivations has been found which preexists conscious understanding and enjoys an autonomous and even protected existence in relation to consciousness.

From this point of view some commentators make a very clear distinction, in the case of psychoanalysis, between the clinical theory, which is situated squarely, despite a certain ambiguity of language, on the level of a practice based on the explanation by reasons, and the metapsychology, which tries to give the construction an inadequate causal infrastructure and describes a hypothetical mental apparatus whose way of functioning is claimed to be purely causal. I have already suggested in the previous chapter why this attempt at reinterpretation constitutes a form of misplaced charity that does justice neither to Freud's intentions nor to the real nature of his theory. Cioffi is certainly right to note that the confusion of reasons and causes in Freud's discourse and enterprise is not accidental but in a way constitutive; it is not just the result, as people have often said, of a simple scientistic misinterpretation on Freud's part with regard to his own interpretive practice. Freud says that "we call a process unconscious if we are obliged to assume that it is being activated *at the moment*, though *at the moment* we known nothing about it" (*New Introductory Lectures*, p. 70). And as Cioffi notes: "Making the reference of his claims an imperceptible process, contemporary with the 'act' it is supposed to explain, enables Freud to combine the compatibility with an agent's candid disavowal of a hypothesis about causes of his behavior, with the vulnerability to counterexample of Collingwood-type reconstructions of an historical agent's grounds for his action" ("Wittgenstein's Freud," p. 195). Hence the hypothetical causal process, when it is recognized, must constitute a reason, and at the same time, like any other process of this kind, it may very well never be recognized or change its status from possible or probable cause to accepted reason. We can even say that what makes unconscious reasons something other than simple causes is precisely the fact that they are known unconsciously, although something prevents this knowledge from becoming conscious, that is, from becoming knowledge in the usual sense. Freud speaks, for example, of a "conscious ignorance and [an] unconscious knowledge of the motivation of accidental psychic events [that] is one of the psychical roots of superstition" (*The Psychopathology of Everyday Life*, p. 258). And he judges that human beings, independently of the latest techniques refined for the scientific exploration of the unconscious, have always possessed an "obscure recognition [which, he says, must not be confused with true knowledge] of psychical factors and relations in the unconscious," a knowledge that is constituted by "the endopsychic perception of these factors and relations." Unavailable in the form of conscious knowledge of this unconscious universe, this perception is reflected on the conscious level in the transposed and ennobled, but inadequate, form of a suprasensible reality. Consciousness, then, is not, as it were, the passage from pure and simple ignorance to knowledge, but rather from a censored, displaced knowledge which has misconstrued its real object, to an actualized knowledge.

Unconscious processes are processes that are supposed to have (really) taken place at a given moment, without the interested party's knowledge. And given what was just said, it is not surprising that Freud says of them, with something close to indifference, that they constitute the determining cause, provide the motive, and contain the meaning of the action to be explained. The language he uses is typically that of a scientist postulating the existence of a hypothetical underlying process to explain certain observable effects. But Wittgenstein maintains that the reality of this process, contrary to appearances, is never really in question, for if it were, the fact that the patient is disposed to accept the psychoanalyst's explanation would certainly not constitute proof that the process effectively took place. Freud says of one of his patients: "It took a fairly long time and called for much labour before she understood and admitted to me that such a motive (*Motiv*) alone could have been the driving force (*die treibende Kraft*) of her obsessional action" (*Introductory Lectures*, p. 277). Wittgenstein objects that discovering a determining cause and agreeing to the existence of a reason or a motive constitute two very different things. And they continue to be different, even when it is allowed that a reason can also be a cause.

CHAPTER V

The Mechanics of the Mind

Everything can be explained by efficient and final causes; but whatever concerns rational substances is explained more naturally by
the consideration of ends, just as what concerns other substances
is explained better by efficient causes.

—G. W. LEIBNIZ

FREUD'S COLOSSAL PREJUDICES, in Wittgenstein's view, all stem from three
underlying assumptions of Freudian theory which he implicitly or explicitly contests. The first of these is psychic determinism, which Freud himself regularly presented as a constitutive preconception that could not be
questioned. As Sulloway writes: "Freud's entire life's work in science was
characterized by an abiding faith in the notion that all vital phenomena,
including psychical ones, are rigidly and lawfully determined by the principle of cause and effect" (*Freud, Biologist of the Mind*, p. 94). In the
Psychopathology of Everyday Life, Freud explains what distinguishes his
basic convictions from those of the superstitious man:

> I do not believe that an event in whose occurrence my mental life plays no
> part can teach me any hidden thing about the future shape of reality; but I
> believe that an unintentional manifestation of my own mental activity *does*
> on the other hand disclose something hidden, though again it is something
> that belongs only to my mental life. I believe in external (real) chance, it is
> true, but not in internal (psychical) chance. With the superstitious person it
> is the other way round. He knows nothing of the motivation of his chance
> actions and parapraxes, and he believes in psychical accidental events; and,
> on the other hand, he has a tendency to ascribe to external chance happenings
> a meaning which will become manifest in real events, and to regard such
> chance happenings as a means of expressing something that is hidden from
> him in the external world. (p. 257)

Of course, as Popper notes,[1] scientific determinism does not simply assert the existence of causes but also holds that the knowledge of these

causes allows us, at least in theory, to predict an event with a high degree of accuracy, so the claim of psychic determinism cannot be much more than a metaphysical principle or a simple methodological postulate. Unlike the thesis of physical determinism, it has never actually managed to go beyond this stage. It is one thing to declare that all mental events are determined by their causes as rigorously as physical events; it is quite another to formulate causal laws appropriate to the subject that would in principle allow us in every case, on the basis of a sufficiently accurate description of the initial conditions, to predict with certainty the precise course of events in mental life. Popper figures that we have no psychological theory available to us (certainly not psychoanalysis) that would allow the articulation of sufficient evidence to make this kind of prediction and to calculate the degree of precision such evidence requires. If we ask ourselves, as Wittgenstein does regarding the thesis of psychophysiological parallelism, what we *really* know about these things, it is difficult not to conclude with Popper that "the idea of using psychological methods to predict a man's action with any desired degree of accuracy is so alien to psychological thought that we have difficulty even grasping its implications. It would imply, for example, the capacity to predict with sufficient accuracy how quickly a man would go upstairs to find a letter informing him of his promotion—or his dismissal" (*The Open Universe*, pp. 23–24). To be honest, we have simply no idea how the knowledge of initial physical conditions might combine with the knowledge of other initial conditions—physiological, psychological, economic, etc.—to make possible a prediction of this kind. But the thesis of psychic determinism evidently does not require that we possess this kind of knowledge. It says simply that the course of mental events and human actions is *conditionally predictable*, meaning that it might be predicted if a certain knowledge, which is logically possible though perhaps factually impossible, existed.

Max Planck, in a lecture on freedom of the will, proposes that when we say an event is causally determined, we mean that in principle a possibility exists for a sufficiently informed observer to predict its occurrence. Independently of questions about the nature and origin of causality, it does seem that a process which can be predicted with certainty is in one way or another causally determined, and conversely, that the causally determined character of a process implies the possibility that it can be foreseen by an observer with a complete knowledge of all the combined circumstances that produce it and make its occurrence inevitable. Under these conditions, the thesis that the law of causality reigns without exception, in the realm of mental as well as physical processes, can be understood in the following way:

> We understand that there would be no question of universal causality if it
> were broken at any place, if consequently even the processes that take place

in conscious and subconscious psychic life, feelings, sensations, thoughts, and finally the will itself were not governed by the law of causality in the sense that has been previously fixed. We allow, then, that even the human will is causally determined, that in all cases where someone is expressing a determined will or making a determined decision, whether spontaneously or after long reflection, a sufficiently perspicacious but entirely passive observer is in position to foresee the behavior of the person concerned. We can represent the thing to ourselves in such a way that before the eye of the knowing observer, the will of the observed results from the convergence of a certain number of motives or impulses, which, in a way that can be conscious or unconscious, operate inside him with different strengths in different directions, and which combine to give a determined result, just as in physics different forces come together with a resulting determined force.[2]

For Planck, the feeling or impression that our actions are made freely is explained by the fact that it is (logically) impossible for the agent simultaneously to act and to occupy the objective position of a neutral observer in relation to his own actions. Nonetheless, the fact remains that motives are to human actions exactly what forces are to the movements of physical objects, and act in the same determined manner:

> The role force plays in nature as the cause of movements is taken here in the world of the mind by motive as the cause of actions, and just as at each moment the movements of a material body flow of necessity from the convergence of differently oriented forces, the actions of man proceed with the same necessity from the interaction of motives that reinforce or oppose each other, and which produce their effect, on the one hand more or less consciously, and on the other in a way of which he is not conscious" ("Kausalgesetz und Willensfreiheit," p. 106).

Planck regards the assumption of the causally determined character of all events as "the basis and starting point of all scientific research, in the historical sciences and in psychology as well" ("Vom Wesen der Willensfreiheit," p. 154). And on this point Freud's position is exactly the same as the physicist's. For him, psychoanalysis has managed to greatly extend our causal understanding of our own behavior by revealing and describing the play of unconscious motives that, combined with conscious motives, produce effects which we were formerly unable to explain and certainly could not foresee. But if we also ask psychology to adopt, insofar as it can, the point of view of the "observer whose gaze penetrates everywhere but who must remain absolutely passive" (ibid.), we see that the condition of passivity may not be honored in the psychoanalytic cure, either by the analyst or a fortiori by the patient. In the complex play of interactions that occurs between doctor and patient in the course of treatment, the position of the analyst is not exactly that of the detached observer who knows but does not intervene; and there is no guarantee that his explanations and predictions will not directly or indirectly influence the behavior he is trying to explain. To this classic objection is added, in Wittgenstein's view, the fact that the patient is never in the situation of the inactive observer seeking, with the psychoanalyst's concurrence, to determine "objectively" the motives of his action, since motives, unlike causes, are not discovered by observation, and what makes the motive a motive depends essentially on the assent of the interested party, who recognizes it as such. This means that his identifiable point of view is clearly not the point of view of the observer who stands outside the process or abstains, insofar as he can, from intervening in any way.

One of the classic and celebrated articulations of the principle of psychic determinism was formulated by Hume: "It is universally allowed," he writes, "that matter, in all its operations, is actuated by a necessary force, and that every natural effect is so precisely determined by the energy of its cause that no other effect, in such particular circumstances, could possibly have resulted from it."[3] And though people feel much more repugnance acknowledging it explicitly, everyone also allows, according to Hume, that there is no difference in kind between the effects of a material and brutal force and the results of will, intention, thought, and intelligence. The connection between motives and voluntary actions is as regular and uniform as anything in the world of natural causes and effects; and the inferences we make from motives to actions rests on the same basis as all other causal inferences, namely the invariable chain of events observed in the past. An action must be considered determined in such a precise way by the nature and energy of its motives that nothing else could result, under the circumstances, from the operation of these motives. Consequently, though we might have the impression of experiencing an inner freedom, "a spectator can commonly infer our actions from our motives and character; and even where he cannot, he concludes in general, that he might, were he perfectly acquainted with every circumstance of our situation and temper, and the most secret springs of our complexion and disposition" (ibid., p. 94n.). The necessity of the action is not, moreover, the result of the agent's direct experience of a necessary connection between motive and action; it usually resides only in the determination, from essentially the spectator's point of view, to infer the existence of the action from certain things that precede it.

If motives are regarded simply as the driving forces of the psyche, it is difficult to understand how they might operate in a fundamentally different way from material forces, and authorize a freedom of choice that these proscribe. But as we have seen, Wittgenstein regards as a deceptive image or characteristic confusion the idea that motives, like causes, can be assimilated to driving forces of a certain type, and so he also rejects the determinism of motives, which has definite meaning only if the motives are simply causes. He thinks, rather, that the thesis of psychic determinism merely corresponds to a deterministic way of thinking about the events of mental life, a way that strikes us as particularly natural and even perhaps obligatory, and is surely encouraged though not compelled by the example of science when it comes to explaining and predicting natural phenomena. The only thing we can say in favor of the idea of mental determinism is that everything in our vision of things points (for the moment) in this direction. We do not wonder whether a mental event, any more than a physical event, does or does not have a cause, but what its cause is. Our attitude on this point could change, however, with the evolution of our scientific knowledge. We might in theory adopt a system in which there are no causes for some events. But "we ought not say that there are no causes in nature, but only that we have a system in which there are no causes. Determinism and indeterminism are properties of a system which are fixed arbitrarily" (*Wittgenstein's Lectures, Cambridge 1932–1935*, p. 16).

To think, as we do from time to time, that our behavior may be determined down to the smallest detail by what are essentially unperceived causes is an experience that has a slightly odd effect on us: "When sometimes I have searched frantically for a key, I have thought: 'If an omniscient being is watching me, he must be laughing at me. What amusement for the Divinity, to see me searching when He knows from the outset.' Suppose I ask: is there any good reason to regard the thing this way?" (Wittgenstein, "Lecture on Freedom of the Will," p. 91). Max Planck explains that:

> The objective way of considering things applied by science corresponds to the point of view of the observer who remains absolutely passive. For him, causal law reigns in all its generality, the human will is, like everything else, strictly determined. This remains valid even for the most refined processes that take place in the world of the mind. Surely, for the causal understanding of creative productions of genius it takes an intelligence of a kind situated at an inconceivable height, of a divine kind, but in the assumption of an intelligence of this sort I do not see any *principielle* difficulty. In the eyes of God, even our greatest heroes of the mind behave like primitive beings. This does nothing to dispel the mystery surrounding these unique personalities for us, or to reduce the sublime heights towards which we direct our gaze when we contemplate them." ("Vom Wesen der Willensfreiheit," p. 164)

In the case of mental determinism, the question is this: Why should we regard all the events of our psychic life as strictly determined by causes which someone might in principle know, a knowledge that would certainly make our intellectual and moral behavior and our way of describing it particularly entertaining for that person as we await a time when we might perhaps have some real knowledge of the causes ourselves? Were it not for the example of the spectacular success achieved in some areas by mechanistic explanation, we might be prepared to regard mental phenomena in an entirely different way. When Geach asks him what to think of Russell's opinion that there must be a microscopic difference between the brains of A and B, when A knows French and B does not, Wittgenstein answers:

> There was an idea that Newtonian mechanics MUST explain everything; and that it must be founded on principles that, so to say, would be sensible laws for a Creator to make (Laws of Minimum This, or Conservation of That). Why this idea? 'Because everything pointed to it.' Everything? No, only everything that they concentrated on. So it isn't (as Lord Russell might say) that *everything* points to the existence of a trace of French in the brain; only everything of the things that fill his mental vision. (*Wittgenstein's Lectures on Philosophical Psychology, 1946–1947*, p. 101).

Risking the accusation of obscurantism, Wittgenstein asks why we should be obliged to regard things in this way. Though at the moment it may seem rather strange and perhaps even somewhat incomprehensible, a different attitude is nonetheless quite possible. To be sure, the thesis of mental determinism does not imply that all mental processes must be considered ultimately reducible to neurophysiology. The possibility of such a reduction would mean simply that the determinism governing psychic processes might one day appear to be only one form or one particular aspect of physical determinism, a supposition that must implicitly confer a certain plausibility on the thesis of mental determinism, as it is usually formulated, but is certainly not implied by this thesis. It has often been remarked that after abandoning the unfortunate attempt represented by the *Project of Scientific Psychology*, Freud himself, though he had insisted on the fact that any theory of the unconscious should be formulated in psychological terms, nonetheless never explicitly contradicted "the belief, implicit in the materialist tradition in which he had grown up, that if only we knew enough, the activities of the unconscious would be regarded as functions of the nervous system."[4] But it is difficult to say to what extent his unwavering conviction of the truth of mental determinism was subordinated to an assumption of this kind. In Wittgenstein's view, the thesis that every mental process must correspond to a neurocerebral process, or perhaps ultimately *is* nothing but such a process,[5] and the thesis of mental determinism have only one point in common: in both cases we postulate that something *must* be there, though we know ridiculously little about what it really is; what we are doing is essentially to adopt a determined *descriptive norm* which, as always in such cases, gives us the impression of being directly imposed by the facts themselves.

In *The Taming of Chance*, Ian Hacking describes a transformation achieved during the second half of the nineteenth century which corresponds to the progressive erosion of determinism and the official recognition of the existence of autonomous laws of chance. "Throughout the Age of Reason," Hacking writes, "chance had been called the superstition of the vulgar. Chance, superstition, vulgarity, unreason were of one piece. The rational man, averting his eyes from such things, could cover chaos with a veil of inexorable laws. The world, it was said, might often look haphazard, but only because we do not know the inevitable workings of its inner springs."[6] By the end of the nineteenth century, the situation had become entirely different: "Toward the end of the century chance had attained the respectability of a Victorian valet, ready to be the loyal servant of the natural, biological and social sciences" (ibid., p. 2). Since according to Hacking the erosion of the determinist conception began in the 1870s, Cassirer's thesis of 1872—the year of Emil Du Bois-Reymond's famous lecture,[7] the virtual invention of determinism—cannot fail to seem utterly paradoxical. Hacking thinks Cassirer is wrong to suggest that people like Laplace, and philosophers like Hume and Kant before him, who were declared partisans of the doctrine of necessity at least with regard to the world of natural phenomena, were able to express themselves only more or less "metaphorically." But the thesis he defends still has the merit of calling our attention to a real and important change that occurred at this time:

> What is of interest in Cassirer's thesis? The first thing is that the word "determinism" was attached to causal necessity between the end of the 1850's and the beginning of the 1870's. Secondly, it was done in a particular context. Bernard in France and Du Bois-Reymond in Germany were physiologists. They denied vitalism and maintained that all living processes submit to the actions of chemistry and electricity (or other things of this kind). The members of the Berlin team extended these physical sciences to the brain itself. Laplace, Kant and Hume were remarkably cautious about anything to do with the brain. You can read Laplace (but not La Mettrie!) as someone who speaks of necessity uniquely in the realm of extended, spatial, material substance. Du Bois-Reymond devoted his life to mental events and maintained a theory of correspondence that approached a theory of identity: cerebral events correspond to, and can even be simply the same as, mental events. This was the project of his lecture of 1872, to include consciousness and freedom in a metaphysics of this kind. In it he declared that we will never understand. We are at the outer limit of possible scientific knowledge, a limit that science cannot breach. Consequently, Cassirer is right on one point that is not simply verbal. The new style of determinism was more imperial than that of Laplace. It was conceived to extend its domination to the brain, the site of mental events. (*The Taming of Chance*, pp. 154-55)

Such a context was highly favorable to the formulation of a thesis like mental determinism, which in many respects constitutes the fundamental assumption of the whole Freudian construct. And it is generally agreed that the emergence of Freud's determinist conviction is due largely to the influence of his teachers, and more generally to the program of biophysics formulated in 1847 by the Berlin group, whose founders were Helmholtz, Ludwig, Brücke, and Du Bois-Reymond himself. I will not launch here into a detailed examination of the genesis and exact meaning of mental determinism in Freud. Hacking cites a reply of Austin's to the question: "There is more than one distinct idea of determinism, isn't there, Professor Austin?" "No," he replied, "less than one." This judgment seems to me on the whole quite justified, and may well be true, in any case, of Freud's use of the concept of "determinism." I will be content, however, simply to make three remarks that allow us to situate his position more clearly in relation to Wittgenstein's. (1) On the problem of chance, Freud acts like a typical man of the Age of Reason for whom chance can be merely an appearance, and the belief in chance, even in mental life where its existence would seem more evident than elsewhere, merely the reflection of an antiscientific and antirational attitude related to obscurantism and superstition (it is significant that Wittgenstein, in contrast, regards as a typically modern superstition the evidence by which science, given enough time, will ultimately explain everything). (2) Even when Freud realized that the theory of the unconscious had to be formulated in a psychological language that might never be retranslated into the language of neurophysiology and ultimately neurophysics, his conviction of the truth of mental determinism was never shaken. (3) He seems to have been quite unaffected by the erosion of determinism mentioned by Hacking, or by the revolutionary discovery that the physical world itself is not deterministic and that the notion of causality must be radically questioned. This idea, which was at the center of the doctrine of necessity subscribed to by classical thinkers and their modern heirs, seems to have been utterly alien to him.

There is clearly a substantial difference between the certainty that mental life itself must be considered wholly governed by the principle of causality and the possibility of formulating precise causal laws that account for what happens. Even if one were tempted to believe that Freud succeeded, as he suggests, in subjecting events that had previously seemed inexplicable or fortuitous to strict causal laws, one would have to concede that the psychoanalyst's claim to possess knowledge of causes is not adequate to authorize the kind of prediction required by Popper's way of understanding the thesis of scientific determinism. At most, with some knowledge of the subject's unconscious gleaned through its particular method, psychoanalysis might be able to suggest that events or behaviors of a certain type (dreams, slips, parapraxes, puns, etc. of a certain kind) are likely to happen, and when they do, to make some of them intelligible.

But to explain, say, the occurrence of this or that particular pun, a number of other factors would obviously have to come into play on which psychoanalysis is silent and we know almost nothing. Under these conditions, it is difficult not to agree with Wittgenstein when he observes that psychoanalysis offers us not a causal explanation but simply a reason for the joke, a reason that satisfies us, which it must do, though it may at first give the opposite impression. What is disconcerting here is the way the psychoanalytic explanation is presented as the only one that might really explain the joke, suggesting that no purely causal explanation, in the usual sense of the term, would actually do; and at the same time, the psychoanalytic explanation is interpreted as being a causal explanation itself, and, what is more, *the* true causal explanation.

As McGuinness writes, apropos the thesis of psychic determinism: "What appears to be a healthy scepticism and hostility to chance as a factor in human affairs is in reality a blind prejudice in favour of one kind of account" ("Freud and Wittgenstein," p. 35). The crucial result of this prejudice is that events which would normally and quite naturally be attributed to chance (or at least considered to implicate chance) must now be described only as events that allow and require an explanation of a very specific sort. Where Freud thinks he has made a major scientific discovery, Wittgenstein thinks he managed chiefly to initiate an entirely characteristic change of attitude and reaction toward the phenomena under consideration. We can easily understand what he means when we read accounts such as the following:

> We made no scruples, for instance, of asking a man at table why he did not use his spoon in the proper way, or why he did such and such a thing in such and such a manner. It was impossible for one to show any degree of hesitation or to make some abrupt pause in speaking without at once being called to account. We had to keep ourselves well in hand, ever ready and alert, for there was no telling when and where there would be a new attack. We had to explain why we whistled or hummed a particular tune or why we made some slip in talking or some mistake in writing. But we were glad to do this if for no other reason than to learn to face the truth.[8]

Wittgenstein suggests that an attitude of this kind might be ultimately closer to superstition than to the rational approach that Freud's discoveries were to have made possible. Freud does succeed in giving the impression that the only choice is either to accept his way of seeing or to resign oneself to ignorance or incomprehension, pure and simple, something no rational being can accept. Wittgenstein thinks that in an area like this, to accept not knowing or not having an explanation or reason is not necessarily proof that rationality is lacking.

It is clear that Wittgenstein does not consider the principle of psychic determinism worth taking seriously apart from its use in psychoanalysis; furthermore, even in cases where psychoanalytic laws of causality might indeed govern the totality of mental phenomena, psychoanalysis still could not claim, in Wittgenstein's view, to have actually discovered laws of this kind. On the sort of explanation Freud proposes in *Jokes and Their Relation to the Unconscious*, he remarks that "Freud transforms the joke into a different form which is recognized by us as an expression of the chain of ideas which led us from one end to another of a joke. An entirely new account of a correct explanation. Not one agreeing with experience, but one accepted. You have to give the explanation that is accepted. This is the whole point of the explanation" (*Lectures and Conversations*, p. 18). On the one hand, as Ronald Clark says, "Mental slips were thus the end product of a chain of events, each related to its predecessor as certainly as the successive stages of a chemical transformation or the interactions of Newtonian physics" (*Freud: The Man and the Cause*, pp. 204–205). But on the other, as Wittgenstein observes, the only thing that could turn this hypothetical causal process into the train of events leading to the slip was its recognition as such by the person concerned.

We might say, of course, that the person who agrees with us about the way things had to happen "suddenly sees the cause (or the causal chain)." But this view would constitute an entirely new conception of what is usually called "knowing the cause." As Wittgenstein writes: "Suppose that you want to speak of causality in the operation of feelings. 'Determinism applies to the mind as truly as to physical things.' This is obscure because when we think of causal laws in physical things we think of *experiments*. We have nothing like this in connexion with feelings and motivation. And yet psychologists want to say: 'There *must* be some law'—although no law has been found. (Freud: 'Do you want to say, gentlemen, that changes in mental phenomena are guided by chance?') Whereas to me the fact that there aren't actually any such laws seems important" (*Lectures and Conversations*, p. 42).

The belief in mental determinism is obviously the prerequisite that justifies Freud's confidence in the so-called method of "free association." As Sulloway observes (*Freud, Biologist of the Mind*, p. 95), there is in fact nothing less "free" than free association. The German expression "freier Einfall" suggests rather the idea of a sort of uncontrolled irruption. Since Freud would maintain that there is nothing truly free in mental life, the chief aim of the technique of free association is to give "free" rein to the spontaneous mechanism of psychic causes and effects, while abstaining as much as possible from influencing it or guiding it in any particular direction. But since in reality free association must also be directed in a crucial way by the psychoanalyst's questions and suggestions, it is clear that it cannot be considered really free in that sense either. At any rate, even the way we have tried to describe the situation conceals an obvious and significant problem. It seems to suggest that when the train of mental representations is under the selective and directive control of critical consciousness, the intervention of this consciousness somehow disorders and falsifies the normal play of psychic causes and effects, thus provoking a rupture in the determinism which in principle governs it. But this, of course, is just appearance. The process of reflected and directed ideation, even if highly complex, must be determined with the same kind of inflexibility as that of free association.

The thesis of mental determinism also provides Freud with a means of relativizing the importance of the psychoanalyst's more or less active intervention in the cure, and of neutralizing the objection based on the phenomena of suggestion. Freud maintains that suggestion could never simply invent manifestations and symptoms that are not already determined by the mechanism of the subject's unconscious as strictly as those that seem to have the advantage of being more spontaneous. The patient's reaction can be precisely guided only in one direction, which is in some sense predetermined for him. Anticipating the objection that the method of free association in no way guarantees that we have found the right explanation of the slip, since something entirely different and perhaps capable of explaining it just as well might have come to mind instead, Freud does not hesitate to make a rather surprising comparison between the results of chemical analysis and those of his own analyses:

> It is strange how little respect you have at bottom for a psychical fact! Imagine that someone had undertaken a chemical analysis of a certain substance and had arrived at a particular weight for one component of it—so and so many milligrams. Certain inferences could be drawn from this weight. Now do you suppose that it would ever occur to a chemist to criticize those inferences on the ground that the isolated substance might equally have had some other weight? Everyone will bow before the fact that this was the weight and none other and will confidently draw his further inferences from it. But when you are faced with the psychical fact that a particular thing occurred to the mind of the person questioned, you will not allow the fact's validity: something else might have occurred to him! You nourish the illusion of there being such a thing as psychical freedom, and you will not give it up. I am sorry to say I disagree categorically over this. (Lecture 3, "Parapraxes (cont.)," *Introductory Lectures*, pp. 48–49)

If what spontaneously came to the patient's mind owes nothing to chance, and nothing else could in fact have come to mind in the circumstances, the explanation based on this psychic fact, Freud claims, is neither optional nor arbitrary, and cannot be simply one possible explanation among others. This is a rather remarkable tour de force: someone believes

in the possibility of other interpretations and suspects that those proposed to him are somewhat arbitrary, and Freud reproaches him quite
simply for lacking respect for "facts"! Freud counters an argument that
invokes what we have agreed to call the freedom (or contingency) of interpretation with the strictly determined character of the facts that have imposed the interpretation.

When Freud says he believes in external (physical) chance but not inner
(psychic) chance, he does not mean that there can be physical events without an identifiable cause but not psychic ones. What he means is rather
that, contrary to the usual beliefs of superstitious peoples, many events of
the external world have no special meaning and reveal nothing particular
to us, whereas all events of the inner world, even the most seemingly trivial, have this kind of meaning and reveal something to the person who
knows how to interpret them. If indeed we call "chance" something that
seems willed but happens accidentally or that results from a mechanism
while appearing intentional, to say that there is no chance in mental life
would mean that either the observed appearance of intentionality is indeed merely appearance while in reality mental life is the product of the
strictest mechanism, or, on the contrary, that everything occurring in the
mind corresponds to an intention, whether manifest or unavowed. To say
that mental events are never the product of chance can be a way of saying
that they are always determined by a finality or an intention. As von
Wright remarks: "If an action can be explained teleologically, it is in a
sense determined, *viz.* determined by certain intentions and cognitive attitudes of men. If every action had a teleological explanation, a *kind* of
universal determinism would reign in the history and the life of societies"
(*Explanation and Understanding*, p. 165).

Freud seems to say, at least at certain moments, that this form of determinism rules the mental life of individuals. The second of his principles or
prejudices that Wittgenstein contests is a noncausal version of psychic determinism, which holds, roughly, that everything in mental life has a
meaning or a finality, answers to a certain intention, has a certain function, etc. The absence of any clear distinction between reasons and causes
means that Freud generally fuses the two versions:

> As you already see, psycho-analysts are marked by a particularly strict be
> lief in the determination (*Determinierung*) of mental life. For them there is
> nothing trivial, nothing arbitrary or haphazard. They expect in every case to
> find sufficient motives (*ausreichende Motivierung*) where, as a rule, no such
> expectation is raised. Indeed, they are prepared to find *several motives*
> (*mehrfache Motivierung*) for one and the same mental occurrence, whereas
> what seems to be our innate craving for causality declares itself satisfied with
> a *single* psychical cause (*Ursache*).[9]

When Freud says he could not believe that "an idea produced by a patient while his attention was on the stretch could be an arbitrary one and unrelated to the idea we were in search of" (ibid., p. 29), he means both that all the events of mental life are determined by antecedent causes, and that they are really motives of some sort. The idea that comes to mind is determined, in the causal sense, by the repressed representation; but at the same time, it signifies it, as Freud describes: "The idea occurring to the patient must be in the nature of an *allusion* to the repressed element, like a representation of it in indirect speech" (ibid., p. 30). The principle of psychic determinism in the second sense claims that everything that happens in the mental world is amenable to an intentional explanation in terms of conscious or unconscious motivation (or the encounter, conflict, and compromise between two kinds of motivation). Because of this confusion of motives and causes we no longer have any very clear idea of Freud's meaning when he claims, without further elaboration, that everything in mental life has a cause. Wittgenstein's objection to Freud's dream theory is that while some elements of the dream may have meaning, this does not necessarily mean that everything in the dream has a meaning; and that the statement: "Everything has a meaning" (in other words, can be interpreted as Freud suggests) is in any case quite different from the statement: "Everything has a cause":

> Suppose you recognize certain things in the dream which can be interpreted in the Freudian manner. Is there any ground at all for assuming that there must be an interpretation for everything else in the dream as well? that it makes any sense to ask what is the right interpretation of the other things there?
>
> Freud asks: "Are you asking me to believe that there is anything which happens without a cause?" But this means nothing. If under "cause" you include things like physiological causes, then we know nothing about these, and in any case they are not relevant to the question of interpretation. Certainly you can't argue from Freud's question to the proposition that everything in the dream must have a cause in the sense of some past event with which it is connected by association in that way. (*Lectures and Conversations*, p. 49)

Wittgenstein views the functionalist, or teleological, version of determinism with the same kind of scepticism he directs toward the properly causal version:

> If some activity is shown to be carried out often for a certain purpose—striking someone to inflict pain—then a hundred to one it is also carried out under other circumstances *not* for that purpose. He may just want to strike him without thinking of inflicting pain at all. The fact that we are inclined to

recognize the hat as a phallic symbol does not mean that the artist was necessarily referring to a phallus in any way when she painted it. (Ibid., p. 44)

I think it might be regarded as a basic law of natural history that wherever something in nature "has a function," "serves a purpose," the same thing can also be found in circumstances where it serves no purpose and is even "dysfunctional."

If dreams sometimes protect sleep, you can count on their sometimes disturbing it; if dream hallucination sometimes serves a *plausible* purpose (of imaginary wish fulfilment), count on its doing the opposite as well. There is no "dynamic theory of dreams." (*Culture and Value*, p. 72)

The principle of determinism which Freud invokes to justify his idea that all the events of mental life mean something hasn't really much to do with determinism or even, strictly speaking, with psychic determinism and the kind of causality that governs it. We might call it the *principle of interpretability*, since it means that all mental events can be interpreted in a certain way that makes them appear to have a meaning, finality, or function. "Nothing in mental life is without a reason" does not mean the same thing as "Nothing is without a cause," for a reason, unlike a cause one can hope to discover, is not real; it is primarily something *given*, and there is no assignable limit a priori to what is likely to be given and accepted as a reason, while a cause is something that must be *discovered* empirically.

The third and last of the prejudices Wittgenstein attributes to Freud need only be recalled briefly at this juncture, since we have already encountered it in many guises. It is quite simply the universalist assumption that any explanation applying to a portion of the facts must have the power to explain the totality of facts; or, if meaning can be given to some mental events which at first seem trivial, it must be possible to assign meaning to all such events, therefore they must all have a meaning, even if it hasn't yet been found.

CHAPTER **VI**

The "Principle of Insufficient Reason" and the Right to Nonsense

What comes to mind at these words? is the question posed by the psychic analyst. But we have the right to turn the tables on him in revolt: what does *not* come to your *own* mind!

—Karl Kraus

Ludwig boltzmann, who considered Darwinian theory a decisive triumph of the "mechanical" in the field of the biological sciences, and who was a declared partisan and enthusiast of determinism in general and of mental determinism in particular, wrote that:

> In nature and in art . . . the mechanical reigns all-powerful, and it reigns in the same way in political and social life. . . . *Bismarck* penetrated the soul of his political adversaries as clearly as the machine technician penetrates the gears of his machine, and knew how to get them to do what he wanted as precisely as the machinist knows what lever to pull. The enthusiastic love of freedom we find in a Cato, a Brutus, a Verrina comes from feelings instilled in their souls by purely mechanical causes; and again, we can explain in mechanical terms how we were satisfied with living in an orderly monarchical State and yet loved to see our sons reading Plutarch and Schiller and thrill to the speeches and acts of inspired republicans. Nor could we change this; but we learn to understand and tolerate it. The god by whose grace kings reign is the fundamental law of the mechanical.[1]

Boltzmann did not believe that the reign of "the almighty mechanical" stops where the mind begins:

> The applicability of the mechanical extends further in the realm of intellectual things than one would suppose at first glance. Who, for instance, wouldn't already have noticed the mechanical character of memory? I often find that in order to recall a single Greek word I will recite a whole series of Homeric verses from memory, and the word immediately pops into place.

> After devoting myself exclusively for some weeks to studying the mechanism
> of Hertz, I wanted to begin a letter to my wife with the words "Liebes Herz,"
> and before I knew it I had written Herz with a tz.

> Everyone knows how frequently the inner alarmclock we have in memory
> leaves us in the lurch unless it is supported by particular mechanisms (a
> knot in the handkerchief, the umbrella hung above the winter suit). On the
> day I had to move to Leipzig, I went to the window as usual to consult the
> thermometer I myself had unscrewed the day before, and exclaimed: "No
> other mechanism of mine functions as badly as my memory, not to say my
> intellect!"

Boltzmann thinks that just as the normal functioning of memory is
explained by purely mechanical principles, its dysfunctionings can be
explained in the same way: by the very imperfect character of the mechanism in question, or the static that occurs when several mechanisms function at the same time. He thinks the slips he reports can be adequately
explained by "mechanical" causes of an entirely ordinary sort: in the
event, the mechanism of memory committed a banal error of reading or
transcription, made possible by the resemblance of two words and the fact
that Hertz's mechanism had been Boltzmann's primary concern for weeks,
making it highly probable that the name "Hertz" would substitute itself in
this awkward way for a word it resembled so closely as to be distinguished
only by the way it is written. We need only one example of this kind to
realize that despite his invocation of the principle of mental determinism,
Freud's explanation of the slip and related phenomena is very different
from a mechanical explanation of the sort Boltzmann has in mind. Who
knows what a psychoanalyst might come up with, contemplating the
"meaning" of a slip like Boltzmann's, and what it might teach us about its
author's unconscious? Boltzmann's point is that if the slip can be explained by banal mechanical causes, there is no particular meaning to
look for. It is true that Freud himself tells us that at times a cigar may
be nothing but a cigar. But the great novelty is that from now on we need
an expert to tell us when a cigar is truly nothing more than what it seems.
It is quite clear, in any case, that the causes Boltzmann has in mind, and
in a more general way all those proposed before Freud by neurophysiolo-
gists, psychologists, psycholinguists, etc., are not sufficient conditions for
the slip, according to Freud, but *Begünstigungen*, predisposing factors
that simply facilitated its occurrence without being adequate to explain it.
Among other drawbacks, these causes have the disadvantage of being
much too general. And just as they do not constitute really sufficient conditions, neither can they be considered necessary conditions. Freud writes
about the slip made by one of his rivals at the Amsterdam Congress, who
wanted to speak of what Breuer and Freud were supposed to have demon-

strated, and said, instead of "Breuer and Freud," "Breuer and I": "My opponent's name bears not the least resemblance to my own. This example, together with many other cases where a slip of the tongue results in one name replacing another, may serve to remind us that such slips can entirely dispense with the assistance afforded by similarity in sound, and can come about with no more support than is provided by hidden factors in the subject matter" (*The Psychopathology of Everyday Life*, p. 86). In other words, the task of the unconscious can certainly be facilitated by a variety of accidental circumstances; nonetheless, in all cases it represents the most indispensable and essential element. If we want to know why a particular slip was committed at a particular moment, we must reflect, in a way that Wittgenstein would say no longer involves the search for causes, on what it expresses and what it reveals.

Wittgenstein judges Freud's explanation of the nature of the joke in the following way:

> As for what Freud says about jokes, he said first that Freud makes the two mistakes (1) of supposing that there is something common to all jokes, and (2) of supposing that this supposed common character is the meaning of "joke." He said it is not true, as Freud supposed, that *all* jokes enable you to do covertly what it would not be seemly to do openly, but that "joke," "proposition," "has a rainbow of meanings." (Moore, "Wittgenstein's Lectures in 1930–33," pp. 316–17)

Considerations of the same kind obviously apply, for Wittgenstein, in the case of slips, parapraxes, "voluntary" forgettings, and so forth. There is no reason to think that there is something that all slips have in common, nor that this something is constituted by the disguised expression of an unconscious intention or desire. We can, of course, decide to regard all slips this way from now on, and find considerable charm in this; but contrary to what Freud suggests, this is not a "scientific" obligation. As McGuinness writes:

> What good then does Freud's account of the origin of these slips (as they occur, say, in memories or quotations) do? It attempts to show why just these errors (and not all the others that would also be possible according to the principles) occurred. But we are not entitled to suppose that there has to be a reason why just these errors occurred, just as we cannot demand a cause for every coincidence. The scribe's liability to certain types of error is activated in a particular case by the state of the weather, the fact that he is tired, and so on. If you insist that inquiry must go until a reason of Freud's sort has been found for every slip, you are expressing a determination to find that sort of explanation and to be content with it and with no other ("Freud and Wittgenstein," p. 35).

Even in the case of events we consider governed by a determinism of the strictly causal type, it happens only rarely that we can explain why a specific event happens rather than some other, different one that seemed at first glance equally possible. But we have faith that a complete knowledge of the causes would eliminate all other possibilities. Freud's way of dealing with the slip is not, according to Wittgenstein, to complete and elaborate the description of possible causes so that the event seems unequivocally determined, incapable of being other than it is, but to resolve a different problem, which is to find a reason that makes the slip intelligible. And since the Freudian reason is a good reason (if it is one) not because it makes the specific event in question more likely or more certain than it would otherwise be, the answer we get to the question *why* this event happens does not prove that it couldn't be entirely explained by ordinary (non-Freudian) causes, if only we had a detailed knowledge of all the causes that could intervene in the specific case. Neither, of course, does it prove the opposite.

On this question McGuinness refers to the book by Timpanaro mentioned above (in chapter 3), whose aim is essentially to show that a good number of the slips[2] for which Freud proposes explanations—explanations that a great many people find more ingenious than really indispensable or convincing—could doubtless be explained much more banally by the sort of principles that account, say, for errors produced in the transmission of texts with the resulting phenomena of alteration and corruption. Timpanaro justifies the decision to devote an entire work to an in-depth discussion of Freud's explanations of slips and other related phenomena as follows: "I think that [these discussions] help to demystify a mode of reasoning which is to be found in other of Freud's works—in particular, *The Interpretation of Dreams* and in general, all those writings which are dominated by the work of 'interpretation,' which belongs to the anti-scientific aspect of psychoanalysis" (*The Freudian Slip*, pp. 11–12). Since what Wittgenstein finds interesting and even fascinating in psychoanalysis is not its supposed kinship with science but, on the contrary, precisely its completely unprecedented character as an art of interpretation, invented and practiced by Freud with an impressive (and at the same time slightly unnerving) virtuosity, the spirit of his critique clearly does not have much in common with Timpanaro's book, whose philosophy is a form of scientism with an overtly Marxist cast. Timpanaro's conviction is that what is arbitrary and erroneous in Freudian explanations is explained chiefly by a kind of hyperpsychologistic bias:

> It is this hyper-psychological bias which is, I think, the principal cause of the arbitrary interpretations to which Freud subjects the "slip," the dream, and everything we do. It is the effort to penetrate *at all times* to an underlying, unpleasant reality arrived at only by dint of a victory over the subject's resis-

tances, which makes him opt in the majority of cases for the interpretation which is most intriguing—and most improbable. We have seen that this hypertrophy of psychologism corresponds on the one hand to a refusal to acknowledge the class division of society and the unhappiness it produces, and on the other to a dissociation of psychology from neurophysiology (and thus to an at least potential anti-materialism). We may now conclude that the sophisms and forced interpretations which we initially characterized as generically anti-scientific can themselves be said to form (if only indirectly) the "ideological" limit of psychoanalysis (ibid., p. 179).

Timpanaro characterizes psychoanalysis as "simultaneously a doctrine that never entirely abandoned certain materialist principles, *and* a metaphysical and even mythological construction" (ibid., p. 184). And he proposes a classical Marxist explanation as to why the second aspect of this doctrine has increasingly dominated the first. But he does not think, as is often done, that Freud abandoned scientific rigor for apriorism only in the final phase of his development. The very strong antiscientific tendencies that increasingly declared themselves later were already clearly in evidence in works like *The Interpretation of Dreams* and *The Psychopathology of Everyday Life*. "It is Freud the interpreter who must first of all be criticized" (ibid., p. 181), that is, precisely the Freud that most interests authors like Ricoeur and Habermas, who judge that Freud has been a victim of a typically scientistic misinterpretation of his own creation. Of course, Timpanaro does not for a moment suspect that the "scientific" explanation he gives and the "science" that provides it might themselves rest largely on the same kind of implicit mythology which is, according to Wittgenstein, at the foundation of every Freudian construction: on the a priori conviction that all the facts in a given category must be amenable to a highly deterministic explanation, which will sooner or later be found. In his "Lecture on Freedom of the Will," Wittgenstein observes that:

> If your attention is attracted for the first time to the fact that the economic state of things has enormous and obvious consequences, whereas such things as people's general states of mind have not, or that it is much easier to prophesy from economic states of things than from a nation's state of mind, it is entirely natural to think that *all* explanations ought to be given as economic explanations of the historical states of things. "A wave of religious enthusiasm has broken over Europe," while in reality it is a simple metaphor. "The crusades had their source in the spirit of chivalry." And you can think, say, of what is happening at this moment. (p. 97)

The Marxist thinkers, who until recently postulated that even an individual's philosophical and epistemological choices must ultimately be amenable to explanation in terms of economic and social causes, positions of class, and "ideological" constraints and limitations imposed from the outside, etc., were simply declaring an unscientific predilection for a certain type of explanation, and surely took much less trouble than Freud to put scientific rigor before apriorism. In the language of Wittgenstein, they confused the adoption of a new form of representation with the production of a new science, certainly as much if not more than Freud did.

It is not, of course, this aspect of Timpanaro's book that is important and interesting in general, and more particularly from a Wittgensteinian point of view, but rather his detailed critique of Freud's needlessly complicated and sometimes perfectly arbitrary explanations of a certain number of slips, omissions, confusions, deformations, forgettings, and inadvertencies of various kinds. In a very Wittgensteinian fashion Timpanaro observes that Freud "elevates to the level of a general rule cases which are *possibly* verifiable on some occasions," but which clearly constitute a negligible minority compared to the innumerable examples that can be explained in a purely "mechanical" way: "Here too, a mania for psychologizing, a conviction that the most trivial error always answers to some 'intention,' leads to the invention of a non-existent—or, what is the same, totally undemonstrable—essence at a level of reality which cannot be investigated" (*The Freudian Slip*, p. 144). Yet it is clear that:

> Whoever embarks on a study of the "slip" with such a strong and unfounded *a priori* conviction of its "essence," or is so anxious to verify it at all possible costs that he takes as axiomatic what is only a working hypothesis, will force any interpretation to attain his ends. We have already seen this occur in the case of *aliquis* and *Signorelli*, and we can find confirmation of it in many other instances. The pages of *The Psychopathology* progressively reveal to us a relationship of antagonism, yet at the same time of collaboration and complementarity between Freud and his "guinea-pigs." (ibid., p. 132)

It is obviously much less important to convince the subject that the explanation proposed for this or that seemingly banal and completely innocent lapse of attention is true than to persuade him that this kind of explanation *must* be true in all possible cases. As soon as the experimenter manages to persuade the subject to share his "axiomatic" conviction that an explanation is necessary and that it can only be this one, there is no great difficulty in getting him to accept even the least plausible and most extravagant interpretations. Freud insists regularly on the psychoanalyst's encounter with the phenomenon of resistance. Wittgenstein reproaches him for being much more discreet about the inevitable counterpart to this resistance: the eager collaboration a subject can provide in all innocence, seduced by such an explanation in exact proportion to the repugnance it inspires.

In *The Psychopathology of Everyday Life*, Freud expresses his hope that "even apparently simple slips of the tongue could be traced to interference by a half-suppressed idea that lies outside the intended context" (p. 83). But a little further on, what began as a simple hope is visibly transformed into a certainty: "The view of slips of the tongue which is advocated here can meet the test even in the most trivial examples. I have repeatedly been able to show that the most insignificant and obvious errors in speaking have their meaning and can be explained in the same way as the more striking instances" (p. 100). He cannot settle for explaining the most striking cases, which may very well call for an explanation of the Freudian type: the same explanation must hold for all cases. When it comes to forgetting proper names, Freud cautiously concludes from the analysis of the *Signorelli* example: "I shall however certainly not venture to affirm that all cases of name-forgetting are to be classed in the same group. There is no question that instances of it exist which are much simpler. We shall, I think, have stated the facts of the case with sufficient caution if we affirm: *By the side of simple cases where proper names are forgotten, there is a type of forgetting which is motivated by repression*" (p. 7). But when it comes to forgetting the word *aliquis*, believing he has demonstrated that it is not accidental, Freud does not hesitate to write: "It seems possible, however, that the appearance of any kind of substitute memory is a constant sign—even though perhaps only a characteristic and revealing sign—of tendentious forgetfulness which is motivated by repression. It would seem that substitutive formation occurs even in cases not marked by the appearance of incorrect names as substitutes, and that in these cases it lies in the intensification of an element that is closely related to the forgotten name" (pp. 12–13, n. 2). In fact, after beginning quite happily by stating that "factors long since recognized as playing the roles of determining causes in the forgetting of a name are complicated, in some cases, by a supplementary *motive*" (p. 9) whose operation he describes, Freud then behaves as though he had really demonstrated that all such forgettings are motivated and require a motive of the kind he indicates. At first there is no question of challenging nonpsychoanalytic explanations which have been proposed to account for slips, notably the interference of things like circulatory difficulties, fatigue, overexcitement, distraction, lack of attention, etc., but simply of completing them. Freud writes: "It is in general not such a common thing for psycho-analysis to *deny* something asserted by other people; as a rule it merely adds something new—though no doubt it occasionally happens that this thing that has hitherto been overlooked and is now brought up as a fresh addition is in fact the essence of the matter" (Lecture 3, *Introductory Lectures*, p. 45). Yet the "essence" of the matter must at the same time be something one feels entitled to postulate as everpresent. If, granting a number of particularly clear cases, "the product of the slip of the tongue may perhaps itself have a right to be regarded as a completely valid psychical act, pursuing an aim of its own,

as a statement with a content and significance," and parapraxis in general
a right to be regarded as an act that is in fact entirely successful, "which
merely took the place of the other act which was the one expected or intended" (Lecture 2, ibid., p. 35), as far as Freud is concerned the conclusion can only be as follows:

> If it turned out, Ladies and Gentlemen, that not only a *few* instances of slips
> of the tongue and of parapraxes in general have a sense, but a considerable
> number of them, the *sense* of parapraxes, of which we have so far heard
> nothing, would inevitably become their most interesting feature and would
> push away other consideration into the background. We should then be able
> to leave all physiological or psycho-physiological factors to one side and de-
> vote ourselves to purely psychological investigation into the *sense*—that is,
> the meaning or purpose—of parapraxes." (Lecture 2, ibid., p. 36)

We understand, then, that psychological, psychophysiological, linguistic, psycholinguistic factors and the like will be relegated to the background in all cases that might come up. The problem is no longer to demonstrate that an error has meaning, but rather to demonstrate that it does
not have one. Asked how he knows whether his explanation of the slip of
the tongue really applies to all possible cases, Freud responds: "I am very
much inclined to think so, and my reason is that every time one investi-
gates an instance of a slip of the tongue an explanation of this kind is
forthcoming. But it is also true that there is no way of proving that a slip
of the tongue cannot occur without this mechanism" (Lecture 3, ibid.,
pp. 44–45). Nor, of course, can one demonstrate the impossibility of finding (or perhaps, more precisely, inventing) a Freudian explanation for a
particular slip. From the consideration of a few typically Freudian cases
we can easily jump, risk free, to the promised Freudianization of *all* cases.

As Timpanaro remarks, the Freudian analysis of slips of the tongue
imposes a false choice which automatically skews the interpretation in the
psychoanalytic direction:

> It consists in a restriction of the opposition *simply* to that between "slips" that
> derive from repression and "slips" due to the displacement of contiguous
> sounds (of the type *toppro* for *troppo*, *battecca* for *bacchetta*). The odd thing
> is that Freud has only that moment quoted a passage from [Wilhelm] Wundt
> in which there is an explicit mention of the existence, in addition to the merely
> phonic "slip," of the "slip" due to substitution of "quite different" words
> which "stand in an associative relation" with the words that the subject
> meant to utter. (*The Freudian Slip*, p. 129)

The kind of associative relation Wundt has in mind should probably be
understood in terms of the traditional association of ideas. But Freud identifies it implicitly with his own association of the disturbed elements of

speech with the disturbing element that issues from the repressed thought. From this fact, as Timpanaro says, "all non-Freudian 'slips,' and not just merely phonic ones (but those due to banalization, to the exchange of synonyms, to the influence of context, and so on), are implicitly discounted" (ibid., pp. 129–30). It is possible, in effect, that neither the phenomena of contamination and substitution resulting from purely phonic resemblances nor associative links of the usual (nonpsychoanalytic) type can suffice to explain a good number of slips. But, despite the position of Freud and his disciples (who use and abuse the demonstration of the "What else can it be?" sort), this does not constitute an argument for the correctness of the psychoanalytic explanation. As Wittgenstein would say, a slip can have multiple causes, more or less banal, most of which may be unperceived; and the inadequacy of the usual causal explanations surely does not oblige us in itself to accept one interpretation rather than another, or to accept any interpretation at all. To argue from a lack of causality to the truth of an intentional explanation is, for Wittgenstein, a typical non sequitur, or more precisely a *metabasis eis allo genos*.

The chief purpose of the Freudian theory of the slip is to establish that numerous phenomena which seem attributable simply to "failures" of a physiological or other sort of mechanism are in reality authentic mental processes. These are (1) *actions* performed by the subject, and not accidental events that happen to him without his participation being implicated in some way or other, and (2) *mental* processes, that is, processes imbued with meaning. In the fourth lecture of the *Introductory Lectures*, "Parapraxes (conclusion)," Freud asks whether the proposition that errors are "psychical acts" means any more than the former statement, that they have a meaning. And he answers: "I think not. I think, rather, that the former assertion is more indefinite and more easily misunderstood" (p. 60). As for knowing exactly what it means to say that slips have meaning and are even rich with meanings, the answer is as follows: "By meaning we understand significance, intention, tendency and a position in a sequel of mental concatenations" (ibid., p. 64). It would seem, then, that the concepts used to characterize slips must be borrowed, for crucial reasons, from the theory of human action in general and are not those used to describe a mechanism that functions in a purely causal manner. We do not ordinarily regard an event that can be explained by purely mechanical causes as an action imbued with meaning and likely to be imputed to an agent. Conversely, an act that can only be explained by its meaning and the intention it expresses does not seem reducible to the simple result of some mechanism. But for reasons we can already imagine, Freud does not dwell on this apparent incompatibility (or regards it as merely apparent), and sees the two statements "Everything in mental life has a cause" and "Everything in mental life has a meaning" as merely two different, but in

practice equivalent, formulations of the same determinist principle. It is
hardly surprising, then, to see certain critics like Timpanaro reproach him
for having been influenced, perhaps more than he would admit, by Franz
Brentano's intentionalist conception of the nature of mental acts, while
others deplore that he wrongly tried to impose on what he believed was a
science of mental events a model of causal explanation essentially borrowed from the natural sciences.

The confusion of recognized reasons and supposed causes is largely responsible for Freud's frequent tendency to proceed as he does in the case
of *aliquis*, where he "exploits in a misleading way the authenticity of a fear
(or desire) that preoccupies the subject and reveals them through associations garnered by a determined bungled action, in order to confer a plausibility to the causal attribution of this bungled action to the fear (or desire)
thus revealed" (Grünbaum, *Foundations of Psychoanalysis*, p. 198). Timpanaro emphasizes that his criticism does not mean that "one should not
seek the most 'individualizing' explanations possible that are consistent
with the scope of any given science" (*The Freudian Slip*, p. 90). It is precisely the necessity of finding such explanations that seems to justify the
links and cooperation between the "humanities" (of which philology is
one) and medicine, and thus also psychiatry, psychology, and other such
disciplines that belong, shall we say, to the category of the "soft sciences"
and aspire to precision. But "individualized explanations, if they are really
to improve on generalized explanations, must satisfy conditions which
Freudianism usually fails to do. Every relationship they posit, every link
they add to the causal chain uniting a symptom to its presumptive original
cause must be, if not amenable to absolute confirmation, at least demon-
strably more probable than other alternative explanations" (ibid.). But
the important point is that it is not "enough, in order to substantiate an
avowed determinism, to assert that every 'slip' has a cause and thereupon
present extravagant causal connections as certain. Even the magician
whom it occurred to me to consult about my sore throat . . . could right-
fully claim to be a 'determinist' in this sense of the term. 'No sore throat
develops by chance,' I might be told, 'there is an evil eye responsible in
every instance'" (ibid., pp. 90–91). As the anthropologists have often remarked (in particular Lévi-Strauss), magical thinking is not characterized by the negation of determinism but rather by the adherence to a universal and particularly strict form of determinism. It excludes chance and
accident in a way that is much more definitive and radical than would the
scientific belief in natural laws that determine the course of events. Timpanaro maintains, rightly, that in Freud's case the determinist convictions
invoked, as they must be, on the level of "abstract science" do not in themselves prevent detailed causal explanations proposed for particular cases

from arising, inspired much less by science, properly speaking, than by "practical magic."

Freud grants the greatest importance in his theory of the slip to the subject's introspective confirmation of the proposed analysis: this is what guarantees that the supposed cause of the slip was indeed its real cause. "I suggest that you shall grant me," Freud writes, "that there can be no doubt of a parapraxis having a sense if the subject himself admits it. *I* will admit in return that we cannot arrive at a direct proof of the suspected sense if the subject refuses us information, and equally, of course, if he is not at hand to give us the information" (Lecture 3, *Introductory Lectures*, p. 50). This is a situation that is certainly not very satisfying if we grant that the subject does not appear to occupy a privileged position or enjoy particular authority when it comes to identifying the causes of his own behavior. People who, like Wittgenstein, think that the subject has no direct experience of the causes of his action, and that knowledge of a cause in any case can only be the product of an inference, are inevitably led to wonder if the subject's acquiescence to the causal reconstruction that finally emerges from the process of free association can constitute a real guarantee that the sought-for cause has indeed been discovered. Why should the causal explanation that satisfies the author of the slip constitute the right explanation, rather than some other, intrinsically plausible explanation which, this time for nonpsychoanalytic reasons, he is not particularly disposed to accept or has no opinion about?

Timpanaro judges that the only really convincing examples treated in *The Psychopathology of Everyday Life* and in the *Introductory Lectures* are the kind he calls verbal *gaffes* (*The Freudian Slip*, p. 104). These are cases in which "it is indeed legitimate to consider the phonic similarity between the two words as a merely subsidiary cause, precisely because this similarity is not *in itself* enough to explain the 'slip.' " (ibid., p. 126). But, he adds,

> we must repeat what we have already said on p. 104 sq.: all the really persuasive examples belong to that type which we have called a *gaffe*. "Slips" of this kind certainly presuppose that something has been suppressed, but the speaker is fully conscious of, and currently preoccupied with, whatever it is that he wants to conceal from those to whom he is speaking. It is not something which has genuinely been "repressed" (forgotten) and re-emerges from the depths of his unconscious. (Ibid., pp. 126–27)

In other words, the Freudian explanation is convincing in cases where the genesis of the slip has nothing specifically Freudian about it. On the other hand, the explanations become increasingly artificial, questionable, and concocted the further they move away from the typical case of the gaffe toward the "slips" that can seem more properly Freudian, in which we must exhume a hidden cause that is deeply buried in the unconscious (cf. ibid., p. 105).

On this point Grünbaum is as skeptical as Timpanaro. The important conclusion is, in his view, this:

> *If there are any slips that are actually caused by genuine repressions, Freud did not give us any good reason to think that his clinical methods can identify and certify their causes as such*, no matter how interesting the elicited "free" associations might otherwise be. As is apparent from my arguments, this adverse upshot seems indefeasible even if one were to grant that the analyst does not influence the subject's "free" associations (*Foundations of Psychoanalysis*, p. 206).

On the other hand, it is certainly possible that even if the psychoanalyst agrees to withhold from the subject the real causes of her action, the method of free association is likely to put her on the track of reasons that the subject will accept in the end, as unpleasant as they might be at first. In answer to the objection that the subject constitutes the final authority when she agrees with the psychoanalyst's reconstruction but doesn't count when she expresses her disagreement, Freud himself proposes the analogy of the judge who treats the accused man's confession as definitive proof of criminality but does not feel compelled to accept his pleas of innocence (cf. *Introductory Lectures*, p. 50). The analogy is a little unsettling because it seems to give aid and comfort to those who have suspected psychoanalysis of using rather inquisitorial methods to extort the confession of things which seem at first to be as unconfessable as an ordinary criminal offense. And this may not be a satisfying response to the objection it is meant to refute. But what is clear is that the assymetry Freud describes and attempts to justify is precisely the kind of thing one must expect if, as Wittgenstein declares, the aim of psychoanalysis is not to identify causes by methods that are really adapted to this kind of enterprise, but rather to suggest convincing reasons. If the subject recognizes one reason as being *her* reason, then it is indeed so; but the fact that at another time she indignantly rejects a motive proposed to explain her action does not necessarily mean that she is right and that the psychoanalyst who proposes it is wrong. The aim of the cure is precisely to produce the kind of transformation that will lead her to consider things from a different angle. But it is not clear that this transformation has been obtained chiefly through a better knowledge of the real causes of her behavior.

CHAPTER VII

The "Message" of the Dream

At that time I learnt how to translate the language of dreams into
the forms of expression of our own thought—language.

—Sigmund Freud, "A Case of Hysteria [Dora]," *SE* 7:15)

Think of how puzzling a dream is. Such a riddle does not *have* a
solution. It intrigues us. It is *as if* there were a riddle here. This
could be a primitive reaction.

—Ludwig Wittgenstein, *Last Writings on the Philosophy of
Psychology*, vol. 1, sec. 195

What if someone were to say: The plot of a dream is a strange
disturbance of memory; it gathers together a great number of
memories from the preceding day, from days before that, even from
childhood, and turns them into the memory of an event which took
place while a person was sleeping. Indeed, all of us are familiar with
instances in which we blend several days' memories into one.

—Ibid., vol. 1, sec. 656

Freud justifies the interest psychoanalysis holds for the sciences of language by invoking a considerably broadened concept of what constitutes
a language:

> For in what follows "speech" must be understood not merely to mean the
> expression of thought in words but to include the speech of gesture and every
> other method, such, for instance, as writing, by which mental activity can be
> expressed. That being so, it may be pointed out that the interpretations made
> by psycho-analysis are first and foremost translations from an alien method
> of expression into one which is familiar to us. When we interpret a dream
> we are simply translating a particular thought-content (the latent dream

thoughts) from the "language of the dreams" into our waking speech. In the course of doing so we learn the peculiarities of this dream language and it is borne in upon us that it forms part of a highly archaic system of expression. Thus, to take an instance, there is no special indication for the negative in the language of dreams. Contraries may stand for each other in the dream's content and may be represented by the same element. Or, we may put it like this: concepts are still ambivalent in dream-language, and unite within themselves contrary meanings—as is the case, according to the hypotheses of philologists, in the oldest roots of historical languages." ("The Claims of Psycho-Analysis" [1913], p. 176)

Wittgenstein openly admits that the elements of the dream can give the impression of saying something we cannot yet understand:

> There seems to be something in dream images that has a certain resemblance to the signs of a language. As a series of marks on paper or on sand might have. There might be no mark which we recognized as a conventional sign in any alphabet we knew, and yet we might have a strong feeling that they must be a language of some sort: that they mean something. There is a cathedral in Moscow with five spires. On each of these there is a different sort of curving configuration. One gets the strong impression that these different shapes and arrangements must mean something. (*Lectures and Conversations*, p. 45)

Does this powerful feeling of being in the presence of something meaningful signify that one is really in the presence of a language in which something meaningful is expressed? Wittgenstein is not convinced that we can speak, as Freud does, of a "language of the dream":

> Suppose you look on a dream as a kind of language. A way of saying something, or a way of symbolizing something. These might be regular, not necessarily alphabetical—it might be like Chinese, say. We might then find a way of translating this symbolism into the language of ordinary speech, ordinary thoughts. But then the translation ought to be possible both ways. It ought to be possible by employing the same technique to translate ordinary thoughts into dream language. As Freud recognizes, this is never done and cannot be done. So we might question whether dreaming is a way of thinking something, whether it is a language at all. (Ibid., p. 48)

There are obvious resemblances between dream images and linguistic signs. But it is only the feeling that we have the power to interpret at least some of them and some of their arrangements that gives us the impression of dealing with a preexisting language, with its vocabulary and rules, which we try to decipher, while normally we know or at least have good reason to suppose that we are dealing with something that *is* a language, a language that we are simply for the moment incapable of translating into ours. If we were sure of dealing with a language, then there would have to be an interpretation, perhaps the only correct interpretation, of the "message" we are trying to understand. But Wittgenstein seriously doubts that we find ourselves in this situation when it comes to the dream:

> Suppose there were a picture in a comic paper, dated shortly after the last war. It might contain one figure of which you would say it was obviously a caricature of Churchill, another figure marked somehow with a hammer and sickle so that you would say it was obviously supposed to be Russia. Suppose the title of the picture was lacking. Still, you might be sure that, in view of the two figures mentioned, the whole picture was obviously trying to make some point about the political situation at that time.
>
> The question is whether you would always be justified in assuming that there is some one joke or some one point which is *the* point which the cartoon is making. Perhaps even the picture as a whole has no "right interpretation" at all. You might say: "There are indications—such as the two figures mentioned—which suggest that it has." And I might answer that perhaps these indications are all that there is. Once you have got an interpretation of these two figures, there may be no ground for saying that there *must* be an interpretation of the whole thing or of every detail of it on similar lines.
>
> The situation may be similar in dreams.
>
> Freud would ask: "What made you hallucinate that situation at all?" One might answer that there need not have been *anything* that *made* me hallucinate it. (*Lectures and Conversations*, pp. 48–49)

Wittgenstein would like us to entertain the possibility that perhaps the enigmatic content of the dream has no meaning and no particular reason, or that it may have a meaning and reason quite different from those Freud suggests. But, as Wittgenstein says, this is just what is so difficult, if not impossible, after reading Freud. The result of Freud's discovery is indeed to lock us into a predetermined possibility, which now appears to be the only one that merits attention; we can no longer see the dream without the need to find a Freudian meaning in it, convinced that it must have one.

Psychoanalytic theory, Freud tells us, was able to prove "that *dreams have a meaning*. . . . The numerous associations produced by the dreamer led to the discovery of a thought-structure . . . which ranked as a completely valid psychical product, and of which the *manifest* dream was no more than a distorted, abbreviated, and misunderstood translation . . . a starting point for the assocations but not for its interpretation" ("An Autobiographical Study," in *SE* 20:43–44). However, Freud was not content to state that every dream has a meaning; he also believed he was authorized to claim that the dream always has a meaning of a specifically determined kind, which is the fulfillment of a wish. In the presentation of the Dora case, he explicitly admits that his theory might have been much more acceptable had he chosen to stick to his first assertion:

> I fancy my theory would have been more certain of general acceptance if I had contented myself with maintaining that every dream had a meaning, which could be discovered by means of a certain process of interpretation; and that when the interpretation had been completed the dream could be replaced by thoughts which would fall into place at an easily recognizable point in the waking mental life of the dreamer. I might then have gone on to say that the meaning of a dream turned out to be of as many different sorts as the processes of waking thought; that in one case it would be a fulfilled wish, in another a realized fear, or again a reflection persisting on into sleep, or an intention (as in the instance of Dora's dream), or a piece of creative thought during sleep, and so on. Such a theory would no doubt have proved attractive from its very simplicity, and it might have been supported by a great many examples of dreams that had been satisfactorily interpreted, as for instance by the one which has been analyzed in these pages.
>
> But instead of this I formulated a generalization according to which the meaning of dreams is limited to a single form, to the representation of *wishes*, and by doing so I aroused a universal inclination to dissent. ("A Case of Hysteria [Dora]," p. 68)

The statement in question does indeed make the theory much easier to attack; but it also enormously simplifies the task of interpretation, since it limits the possibilities of expression of the dream language to a single and unique form of thought: the "optative" form of the (disguised) representation of wishes. This powerful supplementary constraint on interpretation has, according to Wittgenstein, the quality of a "grammatical" rule, and like all such rules it is arbitrary (which does not mean, of course, that it has nothing to do with the facts, but only that it is not imposed by them). But Freud clearly doesn't think of it this way. For him, the dream is not only an enigmatic construction in which we propose to find meaning by adopting rules of interpretation that could in principle be different: it has a determined meaning which we must discover through analysis; and it is the very nature of this meaning that justifies the adoption of the rule, and not the rule that determines a priori the kind of meaning a dream in general *can* have. The transformation of one of the many apparent counterexamples that inevitably present themselves as supplementary confirmation can thus be interpreted each time as a renewed demonstration of the power of the theory. The impression Freud seeks to give is clearly not that a rule conceived as universal in its applications has been applied to all imaginable cases, despite a certain number of foreseen or unforeseen complications, but that a particularly restrictive and therefore quite audacious theoretical assertion has been tested with success on certain highly unlikely examples.

Freud does not doubt that the solution to the analyst's problem of dream interpretation is entirely and unequivocally predetermined. According to him, this problem is comparable to a jigsaw puzzle that can be completed only by fitting all the pieces together in one particular way:

> What makes [the analyst] certain in the end is precisely the complication of the problem before him, which is like the solution of a jigsaw puzzle. A colored picture, pasted upon a thin sheet of wood and fitting exactly into a wooden frame, is cut up into a large number of pieces of the most irregular and crooked shapes. If one succeeds in arranging the confused heap of fragments, each of which bears upon it an unintelligible piece of drawing, so that the picture acquires a meaning, so that there is no gap anywhere in the design, and so that the whole fits into the frame—if all these conditions are fulfilled, then one knows that one has solved the puzzle and that there is no alternative solution. ("Remarks upon the Theory and Practice of Dream Interpretation," p. 143)

The sheer improbability of an arrangement that simultaneously satisfies all the necessary conditions is, in Freud's view, the chief argument in favor of the idea that the reconstruction accomplished by the analysis does indeed correspond to reality and has nothing arbitrary about it, that it could not result simply from the analyst's suggestions. Once the solution is found, even the analysand who strenuously resisted at first is generally inclined to agree that no other solution was possible. Freud considers it utterly improbable that a construction which accommodates so many disparate elements and also has a high degree of overall coherence might owe something essential to favorable but completely fortuitous circumstances intervening in the course of the analysis, to the inventiveness and ingenuity of the analyst, or to his gifts of persuasion. Considered from this point of view, the objection based on the patient's vulnerability to suggestion attributes an exorbitant power to the practitioner, a power he simply does not have.

Freud says, in the case history of the Wolf Man, that the analyst who hears the reproach that infantile scenes reconstructed in the course of analysis are perhaps merely personal fantasies which he succeeded in imposing on the analysand

> will comfort himself by recalling how gradually the construction of this phantasy which he is supposed to have originated came about, and, when all is said and done, how independently of the physician's incentive many points in its development proceeded; how, after a certain phase of the treatment, everything seemed to converge upon it, and how later, in the synthesis, the

most various and remarkable results radiated out from it; how not only the large problems but the smallest peculiarities in the history of the case were cleared up by this single assumption. And he will disclaim the possession of the amount of ingenuity necessary for the concoction of an occurrence which can fulfil all these demands. (*From the History of an Infantile Neurosis*, CP 3:525–26)

The jigsaw puzzle analogy is clearly a false one, for while the puzzle was conceived explicitly with only one predetermined solution, nothing compels us a priori to assume that the fragmentary and disparate psychic material the psychoanalyst has at his disposal can be rearranged and completed in only one way, and that this is the solution imposed by the problem. Wittgenstein himself rather frequently compares the resolution of a philosophical problem to solving a puzzle. But to him this image means essentially that the elements of the problem, like the pieces of the puzzle, are already in our possession and just need to be correctly assembled. In the psychoanalytic case, by contrast, to fill in the gaps in his construction Freud must use hypothetical elements that play an essential role and which, in the absence of any real possibility of independent corroboration, are basically justified by the completeness and cohesion they provide to the whole. Yet the coherence of the reconstructed history, remarkable as it may be, can merely confer at best a presumption of truth, and certainly does not justify the conclusion that it alone is true. All we can say in its favor is that if it were true, it would explain all the pertinent facts. The hypothesis of the primal scene, which constitutes the key to the enigma, can be considered the result of a syllogism, to the effect that if such or such a specific event had taken place at such or such a moment during the subject's childhood, such or such strange things would be explained with relative ease, and that consequently there are good reasons for assuming that it did indeed take place. But this does not take us beyond the stage of formulating a hypothesis whose explanatory power surely does not guarantee its truth. Another important difference is that for Wittgenstein, philosophy involves simply finding *a* satisfying order among our concepts, the order that resolves our problem, while Freud wants at any price to find the real meaning of the phenomena he studies and the unique agency that generates it, not simply one possible meaning among others, that might eventually be obtained from different principles or presuppositions.

(1) *Every* dream has a determined meaning, expressed in a language that must simply be learned to be deciphered; (2) This meaning is *always* the disguised representation of an unconscious wish; (3) *All* the elements of the dream, including those that seem most incongruous, contribute specifically to the meaning of the dream. Understood in this way, Wittgenstein finds such claims questionable, especially because they are presented

as corresponding to major scientific discoveries. If the linguistic analogy is pertinent, it should instantly dissuade us from believing in the existence of a scientific procedure that allows us to determine what the dream *really* means. The meaning of the dream can only be what explains the explanation of the dream. And Freud never at any time demonstrated that the dream, independent of the interpretive technique used to explain it, had a determined meaning that can be conjured only in this way. According to him, "It is quite possible, and highly probable indeed, that the dreamer *does* know what his dream means; *only he does not know that he knows it and for that reason thinks he does not know it*" (Lecture 6, *Introductory Lectures*, p. 101). Not only, then, does the dream have a meaning, but it is a meaning the dreamer himself knows, without knowing that he knows, just as, without knowing it, he masters and uses a language (the language of unconscious mental activity) whose rules he is doesn't, in principle, know. We might say, strictly speaking, that someone who knows the meaning of an expression, in the sense that he is capable of using it correctly, knows it without knowing that he knows it, if we mean by this that he does not generally have any explicit knowledge of the rules that determine its usage. But in the case of the dream, only the interpretation is able to reveal to the subject that he has unwittingly expressed a determined thought in a language he is not conscious of possessing and speaking. The idea that the meaning of the dream was already known (and at the same time unperceived) by the dreamer is thus reduced to a simple way of saying that he can be led not only to accept the psychoanalytic explanation of his dream but also to consider it simply an explicit formulation of something that he "knew" all along.

Wittgenstein emphasizes that the dream is typically the kind of object that gives the impression of "saying" something in a more or less enigmatic mode; and he is not surprised that we are disposed to accept a plausible and ingenious reconstruction of what it might mean. What is more problematic is the idea that what it seems to mean was really said, unbeknownst to the dreamer, at the moment of the dream. Wittgenstein is not at all convinced that a determined method of interpretation exists (the psychoanalytic technique, as it were) that is able, and uniquely so, to reveal to us what the dream really meant when it took place—in Freud's terms, "the underlying and real meaning" of the dream. The kernel of meaning in some way conveyed by the dream needs to be developed and completed; but contrary to what Freud assumes, nothing indicates that the way it can (and, it seems to us, must) be developed is unequivocally determined. Moreover, the fact that we managed to discover, after the fact, a meaning to a (generally) linguistic arrangement which at first sight had none does not prove that it was *employed* with this meaning.

The dream narrative, says Wittgenstein, "forms, as it were, a fragment that makes a *powerful* impression on us (*sometimes* anyway), so that we look for an explanation, for connections" (*Culture and Value*, p. 83). But this does not imply that the questions we would like to ask apropos each of the dream elements always have only one meaning and one answer: "But why did just *these* recollections occur now? Who can say?—It may be connected with our present life, and so too with our wishes, fears, etc.— 'But do you want to say that this phenomenon can only exist in these particular causal surroundings?'—I want to say it does not necessarily have to make sense to speak of discovering its cause" (ibid.).

Wittgenstein notes that: "When a dream is interpreted we might say that it is fitted into a context in which it ceases to be puzzling. In a sense the dreamer re-dreams his dream in surroundings such that its aspect changes" (*Lectures and Conversations*, p. 45). The important point here is that the dream is not simply *analyzed* "scientifically," the way we can, say, analyze a chemical substance to discover its real elements, but in some sense it is dreamt anew in a modified context and thus transformed into another dream, for which it is the point of departure and the pretext. The different things we can be induced to remember when we reflect on the dream change its aspect each time; and all this "still belongs to the dream, in a way" (ibid., p. 46).

The idea that there is a hidden meaning which is *the* meaning of the dream can, in fact, only be the result of a decision about the kind of interpretation we are willing to consider in answer to the question of the dream's meaning. As Wittgenstein says, it is the acknowledgment of the interpretation that determines and defines what we were looking for in our search for meaning (as when we suddenly find the word that tells us exactly what we wanted). Wittgenstein finds no reason to think that Freud's method, combining free association and the suggestions of the psychoanalyst attempting to verify his hypotheses, necessarily leads to the best or the only acceptable result when we follow our impulse to complete the tableau or narrative to which the dream fragment, so tantalizing yet incomprehensible, seems to belong. Freud is convinced he is using scientific methods comparable to those of an archaeologist patiently piecing together an architectural structure from fragments that are usually insignificant, in both senses of the word. But Wittgenstein thinks that the chief aim is a construction that satisfies us, and may turn out to be quite different from the one proposed by Freud.

It all depends on what one considers the criterion for the "right interpretation." And Wittgenstein suspects Freud of using several criteria at once, with no guarantee that they coincide:

> *Freier Einfall* and wish fulfilments. There are various criteria for the right interpretation: e.g., (1) what the analyst says or predicts, on the basis of his previous experience; (2) what the dreamer is led to by *freier Einfall*. It would

be interesting and important if these two generally coincided. But it would be
queer to claim (as Freud seems to) that they *must always* coincide. (*Lectures
and Conversations*, p. 46)

As we have seen, Grünbaum questions whether the method of free association, even if it were really free, can be an appropriate and reliable
means of tracing pathological symptoms back to the pathogenic causes
that produce them. Nor does he think it can lead us along a sure path from
the "normal" symptoms that constitute dreams to the motivations that
explain them. In a discussion on the historical antecedents of psychoanalysis, Freud cites a letter from Schiller to Körner, in which Schiller recom-
mends that anyone who wants to be productive should grant the utmost
importance to ideas that spring to mind spontaneously. Freud specifies,
however, that his systematic use of the method of free association "is not
evidence so much of his 'artistic nature' as of his conviction, almost
amounting to a prejudice, that all mental events are completely determined" ("A Note on the Prehistory of the Technique of Analysis" [1920],
p. 264). "The property of the first idea that comes to mind at the set theme
imposed itself, then," he writes, "as the most immediate and most likely
possibility, which is also confirmed by the experience one has in analysis,
however much enormous resistances make the presumed connection unrecognizable" (ibid.). By virtue of the thesis of psychic determinism, it is
reasonable to assume that the first idea to present itself *must* necessarily
have a thematic link with the designated subject, even if this link may in
certain cases be impossible to recognize. But the problem is that the thematic affiliation of an idea with the subject of the dream narrative does not
necessarily constitute proof of a genetic or causal connection.

Freud is convinced that the production of free associations, taking as
their point of departure the manifest content of the dream, will invariably
lead to the repressed wish at its source. But one of the reasons he thinks
that every dream must originate in a repressed wish is precisely that free
association seems to lead to a repressed wish, even in the case of dreams
that seem manifestly far removed from the satisfaction of any wish. We
may therefore be tempted to object that free association is all too likely to
reveal an element that plays a permanent and important role in the mental
life of the dreamer, but that this is certainly not reason to consider that
element the cause or motive that produced the dream. Despite the seeming
confirmation brought by the analyst's repeated "experiments," it may well
be that the unconscious wish sooner or later revealed by free (or con-
veniently guided) association is *by definition* granted the status of the
sought-for cause or motive.

Wittgenstein doubts that Freud found a way to use free association as
a method of scientific investigation rather than as the essentially "creative" tool used by artists. It is entirely understandable, he thinks, that free

association—or rather association guided in a convenient direction by the judicious suggestions of the psychoanalyst—invariably leads to themes which, like sexuality, occupy a central place in the subject's preoccupations: "The fact is that whenever you are preoccupied with something, with some trouble or with some problem which is a big thing in your life—as sex is, for instance—then no matter what you start from, the association will lead finally and inevitably back to that same theme" (*Lectures and Conversations*, pp. 50–51). Despite Freud's insistence to the contrary, Wittgenstein suspects that not only the theme itself (the dream) but also a certain way of treating it is insidiously imposed by the analyst on the patient. Freud cannot claim, then, as he does, that he found the true causal explanation of the dream. And if the point were rather to find an "aesthetic" explanation, his method would seem to fare no better.

Any idea that springs to mind has, in fact, too many different possible causes for us to be sure that it will always contain a recognizable allusion to its real cause; and conversely, there is no indication that the thing it seems to allude to most powerfully is the determining factor that caused it:

> What goes on in *freier Einfall* is probably conditioned by a whole host of circumstances. There seems to be no reason for saying that it must be conditioned only by the sort of wish in which the analyst is interested and of which he has reason to say that it must have been playing a part. If you want to complete what seems to be a fragment of a picture, you might be advised to give up trying to think hard about what is the most likely way the picture went, and instead simply stare at the picture and make whatever dash first comes into your mind, without thinking. This might in many cases be very fruitful advice to give. But it would be astonishing if it *always* produced the best results. What dashes you make, is likely to be conditioned by everything that is going on about you and within you. And if I knew one of the factors present, this could not tell me with certainty what dash you were going to make. (ibid., p. 47)

Wittgenstein is not persuaded that an explanation of how to complete the picture has been found just because its reconstruction may follow naturally and perhaps even irresistibly along certain lines, or because the result may seem particularly convincing. He is clearly much less impressed than most by the complexity and surprising coherence of some of Freud's interpretations, and by the way he succeeds in putting all the pieces of the puzzle in place; indeed, Wittgenstein treats these qualities more as a strong inducement to believe that Freud's interpretations *should* be true than as proof that they are: "Freud remarks how, after the analysis of it, the dream appears so very logical. And of course it does. You could start with any of the objects on this table—which certainly are not put there through your dream activity—and you could find that they all could be connected in a pattern like that; and the pattern would be logical in the same way" (ibid., p. 51). My reaction on this point is similar to Cioffi's:

> Either Wittgenstein's table was more cluttered than mine or he shared Freud's genius for constructing associative links between two points, for I have not been able to produce patterns anywhere near as convincing as Freud's. But the force of this consideration is weakened if we remember that Freud lays his own table: "the material belonging to a single subject can only be collected piece by piece at various times and in various connexions." ("Wittgenstein's Freud," p. 203)

The other factor that contributes to reducing the improbability, a priori, of producing meaningful patterns among the considered elements is, as Cioffi observes, the elasticity and multiplicity of the rules Freud applied. Before him, certainly no one suspected the possibility of establishing as complicated and coherent a system of logical connections between facts which at first seem unconnected. But it might well be said that if a way of producing such a semblance of logical coherence existed that was inspired by entirely different principles from Freud's, it would surely seem unimaginable to us until the very moment we found it.

One of the longest and most interesting passages Wittgenstein devoted to the problem of psychoanalytic interpretation of the dream is the following, written in 1948:

> In Freudian analysis a dream is dismantled, as it were. It loses its original sense *completely*. We might think of it as of a play enacted on the stage, with a plot that's pretty incomprehensible at times, but at times too quite intelligible, or apparently so; we might then suppose this plot torn into little fragments and each of these given a completely new sense. Or we might think of it in the following way: a picture is drawn on a big sheet of paper which is then so folded that pieces which don't belong together at all in the original picture now appear side by side to form a new picture, which may or may not make sense. (This latter would correspond to the manifest dream, the original picture to the "latent dream thought.")
>
> Now I could imagine that someone seeing the unfolded picture might exclaim "Yes, that's the solution, that's what I dreamed, minus the gaps and distortions." This would then be the solution precisely by virtue of his acknowledging it as such. It's like searching for a word when you are writing and then saying: "*That's* it, *that* expresses what I intended!"—Your acceptance certifies the word as having been found and hence as being the one you were looking for. (In this instance we could really say: we don't know what we are looking for until we have found it—which is like what Russell says about wishing.)

What is intriguing about a dream is not its *causal* connection with events in my life, etc., but rather the impression it gives of being a fragment of a story—a very *vivid* fragment to be sure—the rest of which remains obscure. (We feel like asking: "Where did this figure come from then and what became of it?") What's more, if someone now shows me that this story is not the right one; that in reality it was based on quite a different story, so that I want to exclaim disappointedly "Oh, *that's* how it was?" it really is as though I have been deprived of something. The original story certainly disintegrates now, as the paper is unfolded; the man I saw was taken from over *here*, his words from over *there*, the surroundings in the dream from somewhere else again; but all the same the dream story has a charm of its own, like a painting that attracts and inspires us.

It can certainly be said that contemplation of the dream-image inspires us, that we just *are* inspired. Because if we tell someone else our dream the image will not usually inspire him. The dream affects us as does an idea pregnant with possible developments. (*Culture and Value*, pp. 68–69)

Freud is convinced that the initial image existed unperceived in the mind of the dreamer before the dream work intervened. The folding corresponds to the set of transpositions and deformations imposed on the one hand by the nature of the symbolism available to the dream, and on the other by the action of the censor. Freud carefully distinguishes between these two elements. He specifies that: "Even if there were no dream-censorship dreams would still not be easily intelligible to us, for we should still be faced with the task of translating the symbolic language of dreams into that of our waking thought. Thus symbolism is a second and independent factor in the distortion of dreams, alongside of the dream censorship" (Lecture 10, "Symbolism in Dreams," *Introductory Lectures*, p. 168). But we can assume, he adds, that this symbolism is a tool which the censor finds useful, "in that both serve the same purpose: that of making the dream strange and incomprehensible" (ibid.). With regard to this statement, we can observe that the image of the folded drawing is no doubt more appropriate to the representation of operations such as condensation and displacement than to the transposition into visual images, since this transposition would correspond as a whole more to an effective shift from verbal expression to the drawing itself. (Freud says that "in the dream the latent dream-thoughts are thus transformed into a collection of sensory images and visual scenes" (*New Introductory Lectures*, p. 20).

Interpretation (unfolding) constitutes the complementary procedure by which the dreamwork is undone and the initial image retrieved: "There can be no doubt that by our technique [free association] we have got hold of something for which the dream is a substitute and in which lies the dream's psychic value, but which no longer exhibits its puzzling peculiarities, its strangeness and confusion" (ibid., p. 12). We have thus found both the *true* story of the dream and learned why such a seemingly trivial thing as a dream can, as Wittgenstein says, inspire us so. Wittgenstein's commentary is, among other things, an implicit critique of Freud's realist conception of the nature of the latent thought which preexists the deforming work of the dream and has been reactualized by the interpretation of its manifest content. He does not deny that it can be quite interesting to represent things in this way. But he maintains that this is not merely a form of representation. If we decide to describe things in this manner, we should not forget that the only criterion we have introduced for using this new mode of expression is the specific reaction observed in the subject when a convincing interpretation is proposed to him. What we mean by saying that he was unconsciously expressing something and unconsciously knew the meaning of what he was expressing is not determined beyond what we might formulate by simply saying that he recognizes the proposed translation as constituting the clear and developed expression of the enigmatic and embryonic sense of his dream. We have no clear idea of what it means, generally, to have and express (through the unconscious) an unconscious thought, nor can we simply indicate a particular way of discovering the unconscious thought that someone had and expressed at a given moment. The *Anerkennung* Wittgenstein speaks of is indeed perceived as a kind of *Wiedererkennung*, a recognition of something that one already knew without knowing it. And if we accept Freud's point of view, this is indeed what the *Anerkennung* is. Wittgenstein thinks, however, that rather than corresponding to something whose reality Freud definitively demonstrated, it more closely resembles a mode of expression that seems natural to us but may not be truly comprehensible.

Conclusion

Relations between Wittgenstein and Freud can indeed be treated, following Assoun (cf. *Freud et Wittgenstein*, pp. 13–14), as the confrontation between two types of rationality. The crucial difference, in my view, seems to be that Freud defends a kind of classical scientific rationalism, while Wittgenstein clearly belongs to quite another order of thought. Freud's position in this regard is rather comparable to that of the Vienna Circle, as its members certainly recognized. Moreover, we can see that Freud's attitude toward philosophy, if not, like theirs, the attitude of someone who would criticize it from within in order to reinvigorate and renew it, nonetheless displays the same sort of rationalist optimism. While the members of the Vienna Circle chiefly depend on the virtues of logic and logical analysis to detect and eliminate philosophic illusion (nonsense, to them), Freud seeks the solution (or in any case thinks it is to be sought) in scientific psychology. For his part, Wittgenstein does not believe in either of these possibilities.

But I think that this confrontation above all reveals on Wittgenstein's side a real incompatibility of philosophic humor or temperament. He openly suspects Freud of doing (bad) philosophy under the name of "science," and of elevating the most characteristic vices of ordinary philosophical activity to the level of scientific virtues. Whereas Freud imagines he is being scrupulously scientific in his determination to show that there is basically one kind of dream, joke, slip, etc., Wittgenstein thinks this is precisely the kind of thing one ought to avoid assuming or postulating in philosophy because it is generally the source of the most typical philosophical confusions and intractable problems.

At the same time, his remarks on psychoanalysis effectively illustrate the difficulty of his general position on possible relations between philosophy and the sciences. If he reproaches Freud for a certain number of characteristic "philosophic faults," he also criticizes him for using methods of observation, experimentation, verification, and inference that do not conform to the principles of admissible scientific methodology to which he, in principle, lays claim. And it is not always easy to determine exactly to which of these two categories the inadequacies and weaknesses Wittgenstein believes he has detected in the Freudian construct belong. His general tendency is to consider that if conceptual confusion has been identified as a major obstacle to the constitution or progress of a science, philosophical clarification is generally of limited importance and utility when the scientific status of the discipline is well established, as in mathematics, for example. In the case of a science, properly speaking, it is ultimately scientific practice, and it alone, that is decisive. Philosophical clarity has, as he says, nearly as much importance for the development of science as the light of the sun for the growth of potato seeds. The difficulty with psychoanalysis is that it is hard to know what would be left of such a scientific project once the necessary clarifications have been made. In this case the confusion is not just accidental and ultimately unimportant (except from a strictly philosophic viewpoint); it is, in a way, constitutive. Wittgenstein probably thinks that, as in the case of set theory, there is a "solid kernel" of brilliant concepts that we owe to Freud's genius. But whether or not it was conceived in the original sin of philosophic confusion, set theory is nonetheless a mathematical theory; and Wittgenstein does not think that Freud produced anything that truly resembles a scientific theory.

Contrary to what is sometimes suggested, Wittgenstein certainly does not question the difference between an enterprise that can be qualified as scientific and one that cannot. Everything he says about psychoanalysis presupposes such a difference. Otherwise we should not understand how he feels entitled to regard it as a mythology rather than a science, and to apply to it a form of philosophic critique which a solid scientific discipline would neither require nor permit. What is not so clear is how he might determine whether a scientific treatment of the phenomena concerned is possible and under what conditions, or whether, as some would have it, psychoanalysis may not be scientific but nonetheless constitutes the most scientific, or at any rate the most convincing thing we have, given the nature of the phenomena in question.

As we have seen, Wittgenstein does not believe that the presumed scientificity of psychoanalytic explanations counts for much in the nature of our allegiance to them. The success of psychoanalysis would be inexplicable if these explanations did not have a particular "charm," and if, contrary to what Freud suggests, there were not also an irresistible charm in the destruction of the prejudice: "It can be the fact that the explanation is extremely repellent that pushes you to adopt it" (*Lectures and Conversations*, p. 24). "If you are led by psycho-analysis," he writes, "to say that really you thought so and so, or that really your motive was so and so, this is not a matter of discovery, but of persuasion. In a different way you could have been persuaded of something different. Of course, if psycho-analysis cures your stammer, it cures it, and that is an achievement. One thinks of certain results of psycho-analysis as a discovery Freud made, as apart from something persuaded to you by a psycho-analyst, and I wish to say this is not the case" (p. 27). We should probably make a distinction here between persuasion and suggestion, since it is possible that psychoanalytic explanations possess sufficient "objective" charm to speak for themselves. Freud always vigorously defended himself against succumbing to interventions of this kind. (Though coming from someone who knew more about this topic than most people, his assurance of having always perfectly respected the rules of scientific neutrality cannot fail to seem somewhat naive.) We understand that he may have been rather exasperated at the continual recurrence of this objection based on the phenomenon of suggestion, the word "suggestion" being, he notes, an all-purpose term that generally eliminates the need to ask what suggestion really is, where it comes from, and when it is operative. He thought he had adequately demonstrated that in psychoanalysis, unlike other therapies that employ suggestion, it is accounted for by the theory of transference which controls it and knowingly uses it to obtain a certain amount of mental work from the patient that is indispensable to the cure. But the resolution of the transference also implies that the patient can be persuaded of its real meaning.

Wittgenstein thinks this element of persuasion is crucial. The psychoanalyst who claims that the dream is the disguised realization of a wish is not making a theoretical identification of the sort we are familiar with in science, such as, say, the identification of water with H_2O. It is not that reductive explanations which are really scientific pose no problem of understanding and are never misleading. Wittgenstein thinks this is unfortunately not the case: "While still at school our children get taught that water *consists* of the gases hydrogen and oxygen, sugar of carbon, hydrogen and oxygen. Anyone who doesn't understand is stupid. The most important questions are concealed" (*Culture and Value*, p. 71). But we would certainly not say that the chemist who claims that water consists of two gases is simply trying to *persuade* us to view it in a certain way. Although this identification also poses the question of how something can be what it is and at the same time something that seems at first completely different, there are good reasons for saying that it constitutes a discovery and reveals to us the true nature of water. Wittgenstein maintains that nothing Freud does can be assimilated to a discovery in this sense of the term.

When the psychoanalyst persuades us that "*in reality*, this is that," this means that "there are certain differences that you have been persuaded to ignore" (*Lectures and Conversations*, p. 27). Wittgenstein openly admits that when he tries in philosophy to draw attention to certain differences, he too succumbs to an attempt at persuasion: "If someone says: 'There is no difference,' and I say: 'There is a difference,' I am using persuasion, I am saying 'I do not want you to look at the thing this way'" (ibid.). We know that the author of *Philosophical Investigations* had a particular predilection for the famous adage: "Everything is what it is and not another thing." In a way, he thought this should be philosophy's motto; and this makes the goals of philosophy quite different from those of a theoretical enterprise, whether it is a truly scientific one or, as in Wittgenstein's version of psychoanalysis, simply has the trappings of one. The philosopher is also someone who attempts to persuade you of something and does not succeed in doing so effectively. He tries, say, to get you to admit that Freudian theory proposes and ultimately imposes simply one possible but not obligatory way of considering the objects it deals with. And to this someone can respond with utter incomprehension by saying that psychoanalysis does indeed reveal to us the true nature of the objects in question, which simply means that the person accepts its proffered explanations whole cloth. In philosophy, the need to use persuasion is not a regrettable fault since the philosopher isn't really dealing with a science, while the mistake of psychoanalysis is essentially to believe that it is one. Its mistake is not necessarily to use persuasion the way it does, but rather to refuse to recognize that this is essentially what it is doing and to underestimate the considerable dangers this use involves.

Notes

FOREWORD

1. Jacques Lacan, "Subversion du sujet et dialectique du désir" (lecture in 1960), in *Ecrits* (Paris: Editions du Seuil, 1966), pp. 797–98.
2. Lacan, *De l'équivoque à l'impasse* (Paris: Editions de Minuit, 1986). In English: *The Lacanian Delusion* (New York: Oxford University Press). Obviously, the expression "scientific delirium" is Lacan's.
3. Lacan, "La Science et la vérité," in *Ecrits*, p. 857.
4. Lacan, "L'instance de la lettre dans l'inconscient" (lecture given to philosophy students at the Sorbonne in 1957), in *Ecrits*, p. 527.
5. Louis Althusser, *Lénine et la philosophie* (Paris: Editions Maspero, 1969), p. 25.
6. Bouveresse has devoted an illuminating study to Wittgenstein's remarks on Frazer. See "L'animal cérémoniel: Wittgenstein et l'anthropologie," in Bouveresse, *Ludwig Wittgenstein: Remarques sur le rameau d'or de Frazer* (Paris: Editions L'Age d'Homme), 1982).

PREFACE

1. Jacques Bouveresse, "Wittgenstein face à la psychanalyse," *Austriaca* 21 (November 1985): 49–61.
2. Bouveresse, "Wittgenstein et Freud," in *Vienne au tournant du siècle*, ed. by Latraverse and Moser, pp. 153–77.
3. See Sigmund Freud, "The Sense of Symptoms" (1916), in *Introductory Lectures on Psychoanalysis* (cf. *SE* 16:257). (*Trans. note:* Here I am citing the authorized translation of the revised edition by Joan Rivière.)

CHAPTER I

1. Ludwig Wittgenstein, *Lectures and Conversations on Aesthetics, Psychology and Religious Belief*, ed. Barrett, p. 41.
2. Wittgenstein, *Culture and Value*, ed. von Wright, p. 55.
3. Brian McGuinness, "Freud and Wittgenstein," in *Wittgenstein and His Times*, ed. McGuinness, p. 27.
4. M. O'C. Drury, "Conversations with Wittgenstein," in *Ludwig Wittgenstein, Personal Recollections*, ed. Rhees, p. 168.
5. Cf. S. Stephen Hilmy, *The Later Wittgenstein*, p. 298.

6. Heinrich Neider, "Gespräch mit Heinrich Neider: Persönliche Erinnerungen an den Wiener Kreis," *Conceptus* I (Innsbruck, 1977): 39–40.

7. Stephen Toulmin, "The Unappeased Skeptic," *Times Literary Supplement*, 2–8 September 1988, pp. 947–48.

8. Fania Pascal, "Ludwig Wittgenstein: A Personal Memoir," in *Ludwig Wittgenstein, Personal Recollections*, ed. Rhees, p. 59.

9. Norman Malcolm, *Ludwig Wittgenstein: A Memoir*, pp. 56–57.

10. O. K. Bouwsma, *Wittgenstein: Conversations, 1949–1951*, ed. Craft and Hustwit, p. 36.

11. Sec. 86–93 of "Big Typescript," in *Wittgenstein's Philosophical Occasions, 1912–1951*, ed. by James C. Klagge and Alfred Nordmann.

12. Cf. Sigmund Freud and Joseph Breuer, *Studies on Hysteria, 1893–1895*.

13. Freud compares the method of hypnotic suggestion, which "is not concerned with the origin, strength and meaning of the morbid symptoms" but simply prevents them from manifesting themselves, to the psychoanalytic method which in addition suppresses their causes by resorting to Leonardo da Vinci's two formulas: the first proceeds, like painting, *per via di porre*, and the second, like sculpture, *per via di levare*. Cf. Freud, "On Psychotherapy" (1904), in *Collected Papers* (hereafter, *CP*), ed. Strachey, vol. I, pp. 253–54.

14. On this point, cf. Frank J. Sulloway, *Freud, Biologist of the Mind*.

15. Paul-Laurent Assoun, *Freud et Wittgenstein*, p. 24.

16. Brian McGuinness, "Wittgenstein cent ans après," *Acta du Colloque Wittgenstein* (June 1988), La reception de Wittgenstein sous la direction de Fernando Gil (Editions Trans-Europ-Repress, 1990), p. 77.

17. Brian McGuinness, *Wittgenstein: A Life* I:34.

18. .Cf. Thomas Szasz, *Karl Kraus and the Soul Doctors*, p. 36.

19. Karl Kraus, "Unbefugte Psychologie" (Unauthorized Psychology), in *Werkausgabe*, vol. 4. Cf. also, "Beim Wort Genommen" (Taken by the word): "The new science of the soul has dared to spit on the mystery of genius. If things don't stop at this point where Kleist and Lenau are concerned, then I will stand guard at the door and turn back to the gutter the medical peddlers who go around these days shouting, 'Nothing to treat?' Their theory would like to shrink the personality after expanding irresponsibility. This business is such a private practice that the interested parties must defend themselves as best they can. But we shall withdraw Kleist and Lenau from the consultation!"

20. Freud, *The Future of an Illusion* (1927), ed. Strachey, trans. Robson-Scott, p. 63 (chap. 7).

21. Freud, *Civilization and Its Discontents* (1929), ed. Strachey, trans. Rivière, *SE* 21:28 (chap. 2).

22. Freud, *The Psychopathology of Everyday Life* (1904), *SE* 6:256.

23. Freud, "The Philosophical Interest of Psycho-analysis" (1913), *SE* 13:179.

24. Paul Engelmann, *Letters from Ludwig Wittgenstein*, pp. 55–56.

25. It is true that overinterpretation, which is, to say the least, second nature to disciples of psychoanalytic thinking, allows one to compensate, in a good number of cases, for the lack of facts. Thus, for example, when Wittgenstein in *Philosophical Investigations* (sec. 79) uses the example of Moses (which, for obvious reasons, cannot have been chosen at random) in a discussion of the meaning of proper

names, this inevitably demands a comparison with Freud's essay, *Moses and Monotheism* (cf. Freud, "The Philosophical Interest of Psycho-analysis," p. 218). It is reading things of this sort that allows us to gauge to what extent Wittgenstein's criticisms, whose pertinence and profundity are being celebrated, are in fact absolutely disregarded.

CHAPTER II

1. Cf. Ernest Tugendhat, *Selbstbewusstsein und Selbsbestimmung: Sprachanalytische Interpretationen.*

2. Freud, "The Unconscious" (1915), trans. Joan Rivière, in *CP* 4:104.

3. Freud, *The Ego and the Id* (1927), trans. Rivière, p. 14.

4. Freud, "Resistance and Repression," Lecture 19 in *Introductory Lectures on Psychoanalysis* (Rivière trans.; cf. *SE* 16:296).

5. Kurt Koffka, "On the Structure of the Unconscious," in *The Unconscious: A Symposium*, ed. Dummer, pp. 43–44.

6. *Wittgenstein's Lectures, Cambridge, 1932–1935*, pp. 39–40.

7. Wittgenstein, *The Blue and Brown Books*, pp. 57–58.

8. G. W. Leibniz, *New Essays on Human Understanding*, trans. and ed. by Remnant and Bennett, bk.3, chap. 4, sec. 17, p. 301.

9. Leibniz, "Quid sit idea," in *Philosophische Schriften*, ed. Gerhardt: 7:263.

10. Leibniz, *Opuscules et fragments inédits*, ed. Couturat, p. 37.

11. David Archard, *Consciousness and the Unconscious*, pp. 126–27.

12. P. M. S. Hacker, "Languages, Minds and Brains," in *Mindwaves*, ed. Blakemore and Greenfield, p. 486.

13. Wittgenstein, "Ursache und Wirkung: Intuitives Erfassen," *Philosophia* 6 (1976): 402.

14. On this point, cf. for example Vincent Descombes, "L'inconscient adverbial," *Critique* 449 (October 1984): 775–96.

15. Freud, "Revision of Dream Theory," in *New Introductory Lectures on Psychoanalysis* (1933), *SE* 22.

16. Cf. Freud, "Dostoevsky and Parricide" (1928), in *SE* 20:222.

17. Frank Cioffi, "Wittgenstein's Freud," in *Studies in the Philosophy of Wittgenstein*, ed. Winch, p. 194.

18. The case of the joke is actually rather a special case, since unlike the dream it does not produce compromise but exploits the ambiguities of language to reconcile directly two apparently contradictory demands: the uncontrolled pleasure of nonsense and the critical requirement of meaning. Cf. Freud, *Jokes and Their Relation to the Unconscious* (1905), *SE* 8:161. Freud describes the joke, however, in the same anthropomorphic way as he does the dream, as a kind of jester/servant of two masters, who, by practicing the double game and the double language, succeeds in satisfying both at the same time.

19. Cf. Daniel C. Dennett, "Toward a Cognitive Theory of Consciousness," in *Brainstorms*, pp. 149–73. According to Dennett: "Ryle and Wittgenstein are the preeminent modern theorists of the personal level. In fact, in their different ways they invent the enterprise, by showing that there is work to be done, that there are

questions that arise purely at the personal level, and that one misconceives the questions if one offers sub-personal hypotheses or theories as answers. Typically, readers who do not understand, or accept, these difficult claims see them as evading or missing the point, and complain that neither Ryle nor Wittgenstein had any positive psychological theory to offer at all. That is true: the personal level "theory" of persons is not a psychological theory" (p. 154n.). The difficulty, in Freud's case, would then be that his psychological theory is condemned to be either a personal theory of the subpersonal level or a subpersonal theory of the personal level, and most likely both at the same time.

20. Cf. Anthony Kenny, "The Homunculus Fallacy," in *The Legacy of Wittgenstein*, pp. 125–36. The fallacy consists of using predicates normally applicable only to human beings or to whole animals to certain of their parts (like the brain) or to other apparatuses that are supposed to perform functions of the same kind. This, in effect, is to ignore Wittgenstein's warning: "Only of a living being and what resembles (behaves like) a living human being can one say: it has sensations; it sees; it is blind; hears; is deaf, is conscious or unconscious" (*Philosophical Investigations*, sec. 281).

21. On this point, cf. Grahame Lock, "Analytic Philosophy, Psycho-Analytic Theory and Formalism," *Revue de Synthèse* (April–June 1987): 157–76.

22. Cf. for example, G. P. Baker and P. M. S. Hacker, *Language, Sense and Nonsense*.

CHAPTER III

1. *An Outline of Psychoanalysis*, trans. Strachey, pp. 105–106. For Freud, the consistency and continuity of mental life would not exist or would remain inexplicable if the mental were identified purely and simply with the conscious. The hypothesis of the unconscious plays a role in relation to the series of fragmentary and discontinuous episodes that mental life would be without it, which is analogous to the role of the hypothesis of physical objects in relation to the series of external perceptions. On this point, cf. Max Scheler: "If . . . we drop the utterly obscure psychic 'dispositions' and the hypothesis of an 'unconscious,' as it is called, then the insertion of psychic multiplicity in objective time verges on epiphenomenalism, that is, on the negation of any continuous connection of psychic facts in general. Yet this represents an illusion as great as one that would assume that nature is real only in as much as it is truly perceived" (*Vom Umsturz der Werte, Abhandlungen und Aufsätze*, 5th ed. [Bern and Munich: Francke Verlag, 1972], p. 271). Scheler's proposed solution to the problem is, of course, not Freud's.

2. Freud, "An Autobiographical Study" (1925), in *SE* 20:22.

3. Wittgenstein, *Remarks on Colour*, ed. Anscombe, part 3, sec. 230.

4. Cioffi, " 'Exegetical Myth-Making' in Grünbaum's Indictment of Popper and Exoneration of Freud," in *Mind, Psychoanalysis and Science*, ed. Clark and Wright, pp. 78–79.

5. "Remarks upon the Theory and Practice of Dream Interpretation" (1923), *CP* 5:145.

6. Timpanaro, *The Freudian Slip*, trans. Soper, p. 115.

7. Wittgenstein, *Zettel*, sec. 444.

8. Wittgenstein, *Last Writings on the Philosophy of Psychology*, vol. 1, sec. 38, ed. von Wright et al.

9. G. E. Moore, "Wittgenstein's Lectures in 1930–33," p. 316.

10. "Why War?" (1932), from an exchange of letters between Freud and Albert Einstein, in *CP* 5:283.

11. Freud, *From the History of an Infantile Neurosis* (1918), chap. 4, "The Dream and the Primal Scene," in *CP* 3:518–19.

12. For Wittgenstein, Freud's theory—like Darwin's—is related more to what we can call the "morphological" approach than to causal explanation properly speaking. On this distinction and the way Wittgenstein could be influenced by Goethe and Spengler, cf. Joachim Schulte, *Chor und Gesetz: Wittgenstein im Kontext* (Frankfurt: Suhrkamp Verlag, 1990).

13. Wittgenstein, "Remarks on Frazer's *Golden Bough*," in *Philosophical Occasions, 1912–1951*, ed. Klagge and Nordmann, p. 133.

14. Glymour, *Theory and Evidence*, p. 264.

15. Glymour, "Freud, Kepler and the Clinical Evidence," in *Philosophical Essays on Freud*, ed. Wollheim and Hopkins, p. 14.

16. Grünbaum, *The Foundations of Psychoanalysis*, p. xii.

17. Kraus, "Beim Wort Genommen," p. 81.

18. Masson, *The Assault on Truth*, p. 133.

19. Janik, "Psychoanalysis: Science, Literature, Art?" *Austriaca* 21 (November 1985): 39.

20. On this point, cf. Cioffi, "Freud and the Idea of a Pseudo-Science," in *Explanation in the Behavioral Sciences*, ed. Borger and Cioffi, pp. 480–81.

CHAPTER IV

1. Wittgenstein, "Ursache und Wirkung," p. 392.

2. Schopenhauer, *On the Basis of Morality*, p. 53.

3. Wittgenstein, "Lecture on Freedom of the Will," *Philosophical Investigations* 12, no. 2 (April 1989: Centenary Issue): 86–87.

4. Cf. Davidson, "Actions, Reasons and Causes," in *Essays on Actions and Events*, pp. 9–19.

5. *Wittgenstein's Lectures on Philosophical Psychology, 1946–1947*, pp. 82–83.

6. Davidson, "Freedom to Act," in *Essays on Actions and Events*, p. 79.

7. "Intending," in *Essays on Actions and Events*, p. 89. The restriction "in the right way" is made necessary by the fact that "an agent might have attitudes and beliefs that would rationalize an action, and they might cause him to perform it, and yet because of some anomaly in the causal chain, the action would not be intentional in the expected sense, or perhaps in any sense" (ibid.).

8. Von Wright, *Explanation and Understanding*, p. 8.

9. Davidson, "Paradoxes of Irrationality," in *Philosophical Essays on Freud*, ed. Wollheim and Hopkins, p. 292. For a comparative look at the way the problem

posed by the "paradoxes of irrationality" is resolved by Freudian theory and the functional theory proposed by Davidson respectively, cf. David Pears, *Motivated Irrationality*, chap. 5.

10. Waismann, *Wille und Motiv*, p. 145.

CHAPTER V

1. Cf. Karl R. Popper, *The Open Universe: An Argument for Indeterminism*, cf. pp. 23–24.
2. Planck, "Vom Wesen der Willensfreiheit" (1936), pp. 153–54.
3. Hume, *An Inquiry Concerning Human Understanding*, ed. Selby-Bigge, p. 82.
4. Cited by Ronald W. Clark, *Freud: The Man and the Cause*, p. 155.
5. For a discussion of the problem of psychophysical parallelism, cf. Freud, "Der psycho-physische Parallelismus," from *Zur Auffassung der Aphasien* (1891), in *Studienausgabe* 3:165–67.
6. Hacking, *The Taming of Chance*, p. 1.
7. Emil Du Bois-Reymond, "Über die Grenzen des Naturerkennens," in *Reden von Emil Du Bois-Reymond* (Leipzig, 1886).
8. A. A. Brill (translator of the English version of *The Psychopathology of Everyday Life*), as cited by Clark, *Freud: The Man and the Cause*, p. 205.
9. Freud, "Third Lecture," *Five Lectures on Psychoanalysis*, p. 38.

CHAPTER VI

1. Boltzmann, "Über die Prinzipien der Mechanik," in *Populäre Schriften*, pp. 316–17.
2. In what follows, the word "slips," used without any other qualification, might be considered in a general way a generic designation covering all forms of *Fehllestungen* discussed by Freud: *lapsus linguae, calami, oculi, auris, memoriae*, etc.

Bibliography

Archard, David. *Consciousness and the Unconscious*. La Salle, Ill.: Open Court Publishing, 1984.

Assoun, Paul-Laurent. *Freud et Wittgenstein*, Paris: P.U.F., 1988.

Baker, G. P. and P. M. S. Hacker. *Language, Sense and Nonsense*. Oxford: Blackwell, 1984.

Boltzmann, Ludwig. "Über die Prinzipien der Mechanik." In *Populäre Schriften*. Leipzig: Johann Ambrosius Barth, 1905.

Bouveresse, Jacques. "Wittgenstein et Freud." In *Vienne au tournant du siècle*, ed. François Latraverse and Walter Moser, pp. 153–77. Paris: Albin Michel, 1988.

————. "Wittgenstein face à la psychanalyse," *Austriaca* 21 (November 1985): 49–61.

Bouwsma, O. K. *Wittgenstein: Conversations, 1949–1951*. Edited by J. L. Craft and Ronald E. Hustwit. Indianapolis, Ind.: Hackett, 1986.

Breuer, Josef and Sigmund Freud. *Studies on Hysteria, 1893–1895* (1895). In the *Standard Edition of the Complete Psychological Works of Sigmund Freud*, vol. 2.

Cioffi, Frank. "'Exegetical Myth-Making' in Grünbaum's 'Indictment of Popper and Exoneration of Freud.'" In *Mind, Psychoanalysis and Science*, ed. Peter Clark and Crispin Wright. Oxford: Blackwell, 1988.

————. "Freud and the Idea of a Pseudo-Science." In *Explanation in the Behavioral Sciences*, ed. Robert Borger and Frank Cioffi, pp. 471–98. Cambridge: Cambridge University Press, 1970.

————. "Wittgenstein's Freud." In *Studies in the Philosophy of Wittgenstein*, ed. Winch.

Clark, Ronald W. *Freud: The Man and the Cause*. New York: Random House, 1980.

Davidson, Donald. "Actions, Reasons and Causes." In *Essays on Actions and Events*, pp. 9–19. Oxford: Clarendon Press, 1980.

————. "Freedom to Act." In *Essays on Actions and Events*.

————. "Intending." In *Essays on Actions and Events*.

————. "Paradoxes of Irrationality." In *Philosophical Essays on Freud*, ed. Wollheim and Hopkins.

————. "Psychology as Philosophy." In *Essays on Actions and Events*.

Dennett, Daniel C. *Brainstorms*. Cambridge: MIT Press, 1980; Brighton, Sussex: Harvester, 1981.

————. "Toward a Cognitive Theory of Consciousness." In *Brainstorms*, pp. 149–73.

Descombes, Vincent. "L'inconscient adverbial." *Critique* 449 (October 1984): 775–96.

Drury, M. O'C. "Conversations with Wittgenstein." In *Ludwig Wittgenstein, Personal Recollections*, ed. Rush Rhees. Oxford: Blackwell, 1981.

Engelmann, Paul. *Letters from Ludwig Wittgenstein: With a Memoir*. Oxford: Blackwell, 1967.

Freud, Sigmund. "Analysis, Terminable and Interminable" (1937). In vol. 5 of the *Collected Papers* (hereafter, *CP*). 5 vols. Edited by James Strachey. Translated by Joan Rivière and others. New York: Basic Books, 1959.

———. "An Autobiographical Study" (1925). In vol. 10 in the *Standard Edition of the Complete Psychological Works* (hereafter, *SE*). 3d ed. 23 vols. Edited by James Strachey. Translated by James Strachey and others. London: Hogarth Press, 1953–66.

———. "A Case of Hysteria [Dora]." In *Three Essays on the Theory of Sexuality*, *SE*, vol. 7.

———. *Civilization and Its Discontents* (1929). Translated by Joan Rivière. London: Hogarth Press, 1961; New York: Norton, 1961. *SE*, vol. 21.

———. "The Claims of Psycho-Analysis to the Interest of the Non-Psychological Sciences" (1913). In *SE*, vol. 13.

———. "Construction in Analysis" (1937). In *CP*, vol. 5. New York: Basic Books, 1959.

———. *The Ego and the Id* (1927). Translated by Joan Rivière. London: Hogarth Press, 1947.

———. *Five Lectures on Psychoanalysis* (1910), given at Clark University in Worcester, Mass., in 1909. *SE*, vol. 11.

———. *From the History of an Infantile Neurosis* (the Wolf Man case) (1918). *SE*, vol. 17, and *CP*, vol. 3.

———. *The Future of an Illusion* (1927). Rev. ed. Edited by James Strachey. Translated by W. D. Robson-Scott. New York: Doubleday, 1961.

———. *The Interpretation of Dreams* (1900). *SE*, vols. 4–5.

———. *Introductory Lectures on Psycho-Analysis*. Translated by James Strachey. London: Hogarth Press, 1963. *SE*, vols. 15–16.

———. *Jokes and Their Relation to the Unconscious* (1905). *SE*, vol. 8.

———. *Moses and Monotheism*. Translated by James Strachey. In *SE*, vol. 23.

———. *New Introductory Lectures on Psycho-Analysis* (1933). *SE*, vol. 22.

———. "A Note on the Prehistory of the Technique of Analysis" (1920). In *SE*, vol. 18.

———. "On Psychotherapy" (1904). In *CP*, vol. 1.

———. *An Outline of Psychoanalysis*. Translated by James Strachey. New York: Norton, 1949.

———. "Parapraxes." Lectures 2 and 3 in *Introductory Lectures*, *SE* 15:22–59.

———. "The Philosophical Interest of Psycho-analysis" (1913). In "The Claims of Psycho-Analysis." *SE*, vol. 13.

———. "The Premises and Technique of Interpretation." Lecture 6 in *Introductory Lectures*, *SE* 15:100–112.

———. *The Psychopathology of Everyday Life* (1904). Translated by A. A. Brill. *SE*, vol. 6.

———. "Remarks upon the Theory and Practice of Dream Interpretation" (1923). In *CP*, vol. 5.

————. "Resistance and Repression." Lecture 19 in *Introductory Lectures, SE* 16:286–302.

————. "The Resistances to Psycho-Analysis." In *CP* 5:163–74.

————. "Revision of the Theory of Dreams" (1933). In *New Introductory Lectures. SE*, vol. 22.

————. "The Sense of Symptoms" (1916). Lecture 17 in *Introductory Lectures, SE* 16:257–72.

————. *Studies on Hysteria, 1893–1895* (with Josef Breuer, 1895). *SE*, vol. 2.

————. "Symbolism in Dreams." Lecture 10 in *Introductory Lectures, SE* 15:149–69.

————. "The Unconscious" (1915). In *CP*, vol. 4. London: Hogarth Press, 1950; New York: Basic Books, 1959.

Glymour, Clark. "Freud, Kepler and the Clinical Evidence." In *Philosophical Essays on Freud*, ed. Wollheim and Hopkins.

————. *Theory and Evidence.* Princeton: Princeton University Press, 1980.

Grünbaum, Adolf. *The Foundations of Psychoanalysis: A Philosophical Critique.* Berkeley–Los Angeles–London: University of California Press, 1984.

Hacker, P. M. S. "Languages, Minds and Brains." In *Mindwaves: Thoughts on Intelligence, Identity and Consciousness*, ed. Colin Blakemore and Susan Greenfield. Oxford: Blackwell, 1987.

Hacking, Ian. *The Taming of Chance.* Cambridge: Cambridge University Press, 1990.

Hilmy, S. Stephen. *The Later Wittgenstein: The Emergence of a New Philosophical Method.* Oxford: Blackwell, 1987.

Hume, David. *An Inquiry Concerning Human Understanding.* Edited by L. Selby-Bigge. Oxford: Clarendon Press, 1902.

Janik, Allan. "Psychoanalysis: Science, Literature, Art?" *Austriaca* 21 (November 1985).

Kenny, Anthony. "The Homunculus Fallacy." In *The Legacy of Wittgenstein*, pp. 125–36. Oxford: Blackwell, 1984.

Koffka, Kurt. "On the Structure of the Unconscious." In *The Unconscious: A Symposium*, ed. Ethel Dummer. New York: Knopf, 1928.

Kraus, Karl. "Beim Wort Genommen" (Taken by the word). In vol. 3 of *Werkausgabe* (10 vols). Munich: Kösel-Verlag, 1974.

————. "Unbefugte Psychologie" (Unauthorized Psychology, 1913). In vol. 4 of *Werkausgabe* (10 vols). Munich: Kösel-Verlag, 1974.

Leibniz, G. W. *New Essays on Human Understanding.* Translated and edited by Remnant and Bennett. Cambridge: Cambridge University Press, n.d.

————. *Opuscules et fragments inédits.* Edited by L. Couturat. Hildesheim: Georg Olms, 1966.

————. "Quid sit idea." In *Philosophische Schriften.* Edited by C. J. Gerhardt. Hildesheim: Georg Olms, 1965.

Lock, Grahame. "Analytic Philosophy, Psycho-Analytic Theory and Formalism." *Revue de Synthèse* (April–June 1987): 157–76.

Malcolm, Norman. *Ludwig Wittgenstein: A Memoir; with a Biographical Sketch by Georg Henrik von Wright.* Oxford: Oxford University Press, 1958.

Masson, J. M. *The Assault on Truth: Freud's Suppression of the Seduction Theory.* Harmondsworth, Middlesex: Penguin, 1984.

McGuinness, Brian. "Freud and Wittgenstein." In *Wittgenstein and His Times*, ed. McGuinness. Oxford: Blackwell, 1981.

―――. *Wittgenstein: A Life*. 2 vols. Vol. 1, *Young Ludwig, 1889–1921*. London: Duckworth, 1988.

Moore, G. E. "Wittgenstein's Lectures in 1930–33." In Moore, *Philosophical Papers*. London: Allen and Unwin, 1959.

Neider, Heinrich. "Gespräch mit Heinrich Neider: Persönliche Erinnerungen an den Wiener Kreis." *Conceptus* 1 (Innsbruck, 1977).

Pascal, Fania. "Ludwig Wittgenstein: A Personal Memoir." In *Ludwig Wittgenstein, Personal Recollections*, ed. Rhees.

Pears, David. *Motivated Irrationality*, Oxford: Clarendon Press, 1984.

Planck, Max. "Kausalgesetz und Willensfreiheit." In *Vom Wesen der Willensfreiheit und andere Vortage*. Frankfurt: Fischer Taschenbuch Verlag, 1990.

―――. "Vom Wesen der Willensfreiheit" (1936). In *Vom Wesen der Willensfreiheit*.

Popper, Karl R. *The Open Universe: An Argument for Indeterminism*. London: Routledge and Hutchinson, 1982.

Rhees, Rush, ed. *Ludwig Wittgenstein, Personal Recollections*. Oxford: Blackwell, 1981.

Schopenhauer, Arthur. *On the Basis of Morality* (Über die vierfache Wurzel des Satzes vom zureichenden Grunde). Translated by E. F. J. Payne. Indianapolis, Ind.: Bobbs-Merrill, 1965.

Sulloway, Frank J. *Freud, Biologist of the Mind: Beyond the Psychoanalytical Legend*. New York: Basic Books, 1979.

Szasz, Thomas. *Karl Kraus and the Soul Doctors: A Pioneer and His Critique of Psychiatry and Psychoanalysis*. Baton Rouge: Louisiana State University Press, 1976.

―――. Timpanaro, Sebastiano. *The Freudian Slip*. Translated by Kate Soper. Atlantic Highlands, N.J.: Humanities Press, 1976.

Toulmin, Stephen. "The Unappeased Skeptic," *Times Literary Supplement*, 2–8 September 1988, pp. 947–48.

Tugendhat, Ernest. *Selbstbewusstsein und Selbsbestimmung: Sprachanalytische Interpretationen*. Frankfurt: Suhrkamp Verlag, 1979.

Von Wright, G. H. *Explanation and Understanding*. London: Routledge and Kegan Paul, 1971.

Waismann, Friedrich. *Wille und Motiv: Zwei Abhandlungen über Ethik und Handlungstheorie*. Stuttgart: Philipp Reclam Jun., 1983.

Winch, Peter, ed. *Studies in the Philosophy of Wittgenstein*. London: Routledge and Kegan Paul, 1969.

Wittgenstein, Ludwig. "Big Typescript." In *Philosophical Occasions, 1912–1951*, ed. Klagge and Nordmann.

―――. *The Blue and Brown Books*. Oxford: Blackwell, 1958.

―――. "Conversations on Freud." In *Lectures and Conversations*, ed. Barrett.

―――. *Culture and Value* (Vermischte Bemerkungen). Edited by G. H. von Wright. Translated by Peter Winch. Oxford: Blackwell, 1978.

―――. *Last Writings on the Philosophy of Psychology*. Edited by G. H. von Wright et al. Chicago: University of Chicago Press, 1982.

———. "Lecture on Freedom of the Will." *Philosophical Investigations* 12, no. 2 (April 1989: Centenary Issue).

———. *Lectures and Conversations on Aesthetics, Psychology and Religious Belief.* Edited by Cyril Barrett. Oxford: Blackwell, 1966.

———. *Philosophical Grammar.* Edited by Rush Rhees. Berkeley: University of California Press, 1974.

———. *Philosophical Investigations.* Oxford: Blackwell, 1953.

———. *Philosophical Occasions, 1912–1951.* Edited by James C. Klagge and Alfred Nordmann. Indianapolis and Cambridge: Hackett, 1993.

———. *Remarks on Colour.* Edited by G. E. M. Anscombe. Berkeley: University of California Press, 1977.

———. "Remarks on Frazer's *Golden Bough.*" In *Philosophical Occasions, 1912–1951,* ed. Klagge and Nordmann.

———. *Remarks on the Philosophy of Psychology, 1946–1947.* See *Wittgenstein's Lectures on Philosophical Psychology, 1946–1947.*

———. *Tractatus logico-Philosophicus.* London: Routledge and Kegan Paul, 1974.

———. "Ursache und Wirkung: Intuitives Erfassen." *Philosophia* (Philosophical Quarterly of Israel) 6 (1976).

Wittgenstein's Lectures, Cambridge 1932–1935: From the Notes of Alice Ambrose and Margaret MacDonald. Edited by Alice Ambrose. Oxford: Blackwell, 1979.

———. *Wittgenstein's Lectures on Philosophical Psychology, 1946–1947.* Notes by P. T. Geach, K. J. Shah, and A. C. Jackson. Edited by P. T. Geach. New York and London: Harvester-Wheatsheaf, 1988.

———. *Zettel.* Oxford: Blackwell, 1967.

Wollheim, Richard and James Hopkins, eds. *Philosophical Essays on Freud.* Cambridge: Cambridge University Press, 1982.

Index